"Donna Bond takes us on her life's a [...] riences and real-life stories of transfo [...] learns to embrace her own "original wisdom" of what is true inside of her. Donna demonstrates how working with the Principles and Practices of Spiritual Psychology which she learned at the University of Santa Monica, has informed her own way of being and assisted her in discovering her life's purpose. Through developing her own practices, Donna assists readers in awakening to their "original wisdom" and to the opportunity for each individual's Light within to shine brightly. This is a book for those on their own journey of Awakening."

~Drs. Ron and Mary Hulnick,
Co-Directors & Founding Faculty
University of Santa Monica

"Come along with Donna as she intimately shares with you her transformative spiritual journey, one that turned an ordinary life into an extraordinary one of success, abundance, and love."

~James Van Praagh
Spiritual Teacher, Best-Selling Author

"*Original Wisdom* will wake up women. It's life-changing and, not coincidentally, right on time. This is self-love for the modern woman. A real accounting that tugs at the reality of our human experience, giving knock-you-on-your-ass reminders about how thoughts become things. It will make you question everything while illuminating the path to the ultimate knowing, our collective quest: I am."

~Erin Ashby
Owner and Chief Marketing Officer
of Suade Marketing

"To make positive change, you must have the courage to acknowledge and tackle your hidden fears. With her inspirational book, Donna Bond takes you on a personal growth journey so you can dream big AND fearlessly achieve your goals."

~Robin Toft
Founder & Chairman We Can Rise, Inc.

"A beautiful memoir with down-and-dirty life experiences that could not be more perfect for these times. Eloquently written. Heartfelt and honest. Donna is a master at bringing the spiritual and the magical into practical expression. A must-read for anyone curious and/or ready to take charge of their own well-being."

~ Dr. Heidi Zappone
Functional Medicine Expert, Chiropractor,
Certified Clinical Nutritionist, Birth Doula

"Donna Bond brings immense compassion and wisdom to helping us see the infinite power we all possess, which is our very birthright, and the realization of it is indeed a second birth that she gently guides us through, helping us reach our fullest potential as multidimensional beings."

~Scott Ware
Publisher of *Radiance* Magazine and
Radiance Multidimensional Media

"What do you love about the sun rising? Donna Bond's book *Original Wisdom* reads as the sunrise to the Soul. Her words, which are filled with depth, honesty, and heart, will be emblazoned within your Spirit forevermore. There is no need to live a life of quiet desperation, as Thoreau eluded, and this book shows us the way to the entelechy of our truest natures with easeful grace. She reminds us that familiarity is overrated and guides us to the actionable meaning of our existence, wherein greater fulfillment, results, and joy await each of us, regardless of circumstance. I encourage you to read this book, savor it like a warm cup of tea, and sip it into the cells of your magnificent way of being."

~**Stephen McGhee**
Leadership Guide and Advisor
Author of *Get Real: A Vital Breakthrough on Your Life and Leadership*

"Donna Bond is truly one of the finest coaches, teachers, and leaders of our time. She has a particular skill for pulling together the professional and the Spiritual, the masculine and the feminine, and the esoteric and the practical. In *Original Wisdom*, Donna weaves stories from her fascinating life with Spiritual principles in order to provide resonant guidance that is sure to benefit the reader."

~**Ed Adams**
Author of *Step Forward, Dear One*

"*Original Wisdom* has the power to connect you to the part of you where everything is possible. Donna has masterfully made it possible for you, if you are interested in experiencing an extraordinary life, to follow along and learn to heal all that disconnects you from the power of the authentic you. This book is truly a gift for all seekers everywhere."

~**Sanya Bari, M.Ed., LPC, NCC**
Therapist and Coach

"When one has led a life of the mystical and miraculous, what follows is the call to share that wisdom. Donna offers a bite of that knowledge in the delightful form of personal stories as well as the well-researched teachings of the masters in areas ranging from metaphysics to psychology to the mystical. She invites her readers to step off the corporate ladder—or any ladder, for that matter—and pick up the mirror of truth, genuine purpose, and transformation. With actionable lessons as well as side notes inviting the mind to open up to the reality of what was once considered pure fantasy, *Original Wisdom* can be read straight through or savored as one golden "aha" apple at a time. For anyone new to the spiritual realms, this is a wonderful place to begin a journey, test the waters, and experience the best-of-the-best concepts and practices available today."

~Joanne Menon
Spiritual & Creative Wellness Consultant & Coach

"Fiction books have the power to entangle you in the stories of the characters, whereas non-fiction tends to offer solutions to life challenges. Donna's *Original Wisdom: Harness the Power of the Authentic You* gracefully combines both the storytelling and the life wisdom. The book provides powerful exercises and easy-to-read-and-follow guidance and personal insight, and it's a wonderful read for anybody looking for assistance on their life's journey."

~Olga Anna Peddie
Founder and CDO of DM Tipping Point

"Many people see "being human" as something we are, but the REALLY important part of ourselves is our Divinity. Donna absolutely celebrates our humanity. She challenged me to open my heart to ME being human—all the parts of it, even the messy ones. And as I did, a new joy swept through me. I did not realize how much I had just been "putting up with" being human. I have fun, and I have a lot of love and support in my life, but being human was "just something I had to be" in order to be here. Donna's book changed that. I now celebrate my humanity, which allows me to experience more joy and connection between my personality/body and the part of me that is Bigger. So much heaviness is gone, and I didn't even know I was carrying it around. Her celebration of our humanity AND our Divinity, along with her clarity on how they can "work together" for our benefit, is life-changing!"

~John J. Hruby, MA
Professional Life & Creativity Coach
Author of *Space Spiders on Prom Day*

Original Wisdom

Harness the Power
of the Authentic You

Donna Bond, M.A.

The author or the publisher of this book does not engage in rendering professional advice or services to the individual reader. The ideas, procedures, techniques, and suggestions contained in this book are not intended as a substitute for consulting with your physician or mental health professional. The intent of the author is to offer information for a general nature to help you in your quest for overall health and well-being. Neither the author nor the publisher shall be liable or responsible for any loss or damage allegedly arising from any information or suggestion in this book.

The views and opinions expressed in this book are those of the author and do not necessarily reflect the official policy or position of Halo Publishing International. Any content provided by our authors are of their opinion and are not intended to malign any religion, ethnic group, club, organization, company, individual or anyone or anything.

Cover & Page Design/Layout: Paul Bond
Cover Image: Ashley Strong Photography
Additional Page Layout: Halo Publishing International
Editors: Lara Asher, John Hruby

The following authors and their publishers have generously granted permission to include excerpts from the following:

Material in this book is based on the principles and practices of Spiritual Psychology as taught by Drs. Ron and Mary Hulnick at the University of Santa Monica. For more information, please visit www.universityofsantamonica.edu.

The poem "Risk" by Elizabeth Appel, which appears on page 4 in chapter one and again on page 205 in chapter eleven, was reprinted with permission from the author. www.readelizabeth.com

The quote from Wayne Dyer's Wishes Fulfilled: Mastering the Art of Manifesting, ©2013, which appears on page 147 in chapter eight, was reprinted with permission from Hay House, Inc., Carlsbad, CA.

Material from Dr. Joe Dispenza's Breaking the Habit of Being Yourself, ©2012, which appears on page 24 in chapter two, was reprinted with permission from Hay House, Inc., Carlsbad, CA.

Ten percent of the book sales from Original Wisdom: Harness the Power of the Authentic You will be donated, in gratitude and love, to the University of Santa Monica, the Worldwide Center for the Study & Practice of Spiritual Psychology®.

ISBN: 978-1-61244-955-5
LCCN: 2020925238

Halo Publishing International, LLC
8000 W Interstate 10, Suite 600
San Antonio, Texas 78230
www.halopublishing.com

Printed and bound in the United States of America

This book is dedicated to all the seekers
and all the finders of the great mystery.
Each moment of our Becoming
is birthed from our Beingness.
Remember who you are.

Contents

Foreword

Welcome to *Original Wisdom* – a fabulous guide to listening to your authentic voice, to making wise choices, and to living an inspired life.

I first met Donna Bond in July of 2015, when I was teaching a five-day masterclass on Spiritual Psychology for the University of Santa Monica. We met again when I spoke at Donna's USM graduation ceremony, where she received her M.A. in Spiritual Psychology.

Two years later, Donna enrolled in my six-month Success Intelligence Mastermind program, which was when we really got to know each other. Donna has taken several courses with me since then, including a Hay House Writers Workshop, which was when she first shared her vision for this book with me.

In *Original Wisdom*, Donna shares her story of how she transformed her life. She tells us how, at the age of forty-five, she "woke up" at the top of her game and how *she let the spirit girl out of the closet* (to use her words). She shifted her mindset from "having a career" to "living her purpose." She swapped a corporate ladder for a spiritual path.

How did Donna do this? In short, she followed her original wisdom. By asking herself, "What is true for me?" she learned how to recognize and trust her authentic voice. Donna, aka the spirit girl, befriended her wise woman within and learned how to live life in a new way - full of imagination, courage, and love.

Donna's journey of transformation became the catalyst for her work in coaching and leadership. Today, she mentors individuals and corporations to harness their original wisdom so as to grow and prosper. Her work is a blessing and a great gift to us all.

And now *Original Wisdom* is published. Donna Bond's first book. I am so happy to see this book in the world at this time.

The challenges we face today – both in our personal lives and on our planet – require not more effort, but more wisdom. This is a central teaching of my work with Success Intelligence.

Wisdom is our great need today. To survive and thrive – both individually and collectively – we need to re-learn how to be wise.

We are all blessed with original wisdom. We ignore it at our peril. It saves us every time we follow it.

Now is time to wake up to our original wisdom if we are to transform our lives and save our planet. Donna Bond woke up in the middle of her life from a long sleep. And now she is our trusted guide to help us to do the same.

Welcome to *Original Wisdom*. Turn the pages slowly and deliberately. Enjoy the powerful storytelling and do the exercises. Listen to your authentic voice as you do so. Be wise, be brave, and be the original you!

Robert Holden
February 2021, London
Author of *Authentic Success, Shift Happens!* and
Finding Love Everywhere.

Introduction

"If you bring forth what is within you, what you bring forth will save you. If you do not bring forth what is within you, what you do not bring forth will destroy you."

~ Gnostic Gospel of Thomas, Verse 70

It's incredible how many decisions you make at an early age. You make them based on your life's circumstances at the time and they get seeded into your psyche. You often spend your entire life carrying some big misunderstandings within you that got created by decisions you made at an early age.

I was five. I didn't know it then, but I was having my first spiritual experience. I was in kindergarten. As a class project, each kid planted an apple seed in a small container and watched it grow over time. Each day in class, we tended to those plants. We loved them into existence, and with every passing day my little seed seemed to take root and grow taller and stronger. My tree grew so well that when it got to be one foot high, I took it home. My mom helped me transplant it in our backyard.

As I grew that tree, I was also having my first experience with my powers of creation. I freaking loved that tree. We were connected. The pride I felt swelled in my heart as I engaged with my blossoming seedling. Every day, I went out back to visit my creation. I talked to it and I was sure it was whispering the secrets of the Universe to me. I offered it my unconditional love as I sat there in the dirt day after day, visiting with my little tree. I dreamed of the big red apples that I imagined would fall off those branches one day.

On a cool Saturday afternoon in October, just as the leaves on the big oaks in the backyard were turning garnet red, my dad was outside cutting the lawn. His efforts were careless as he was in a mad rush to get inside and watch the football game that had just started on TV. With a cigarette hanging out of his mouth, distracted in thought, he unknowingly and unconsciously pushed his lawn mower right over my little creation. He killed my tree.

I sobbed when my mother told me, as she desperately tried to console me. It was a scene. I did not understand until much later that this event seeded within me the belief that the outside world could sabotage my powers of creation.

Years later this incident returned to my memory. I realized this experience seeded the deep-rooted belief inside of me that my contributions, cultivations, and efforts were not fully valued. It also began a pattern in my life where I had to be the one to "get things done." If I didn't, clearly, no one else was capable. Even deeper still, this seemingly insignificant event, stunted my powers as a creator also locking in the incorrect belief that I shouldn't bother. (Of course, all of these thoughts were in my subconscious and caused me to live a life I really didn't love. It wasn't until I was in my forties that all of this came to light.)

This early apple episode also underscored another limiting belief: *I have to work really hard to prove myself to everyone about everything, because anyone could easily come by and mow over my efforts, and it would all be for naught.* In that moment, the control freak inside of me was born. Thanks, Dad.

Sound familiar? I'm sure you have your own story. Maybe you've figured it out already. Maybe you're in the process of realizing it now. Or maybe you're sure you don't have anything like this running around in *your* subconscious.

What I didn't realize in the midst of my emotional trauma—and in my young and inexperienced mind—was that *the seed was still tucked away* safely in the ground. It was simply waiting for me to notice it and nurture it. It was never truly lost or killed.

Forty years later, and half-way around the world, I had a profound realization. Stumbling accidentally into the apple orchard at the Abbey in Glastonbury, England I found myself on my knees, amidst piles of apples weeping in gratitude. I wept as I remembered and reclaimed my powers as a creator.

This true-life story became my personal metaphor for the natural expression of our seeds of creation and how, in an instant, it can *appear* as if life has destroyed them. But the truth is, the seed is always there. The mysterious energy called the Life Force is the secret ingredient that transforms that apple seed into a flower and the flower into a fruit—or in my case, an entire apple orchard. Growing requires not only sun, water, soil, and the ever-present Life Force, but it also requires—and this is most important—our patience, attention and cultivation. It requires our nurturing and *our Love.*

This book is about waking up what is safely buried inside of you. It's about calling it out into the world and harnessing the power of your own Life Force. I will walk you through integrating the magnificence of your inherent wisdom more fully into your life, acknowledging your divinity, honoring your humanness, and loving your sweet self. This book will show you that you are so much more than what you've been taught to believe. You are an orchard. Far more than a single seed. You are a drop of All That Is.

My Deep Discontent

In my mid-forties, I seemingly "had it all," so why was I so miserable? For some reason, heading out each day to my high-powered corporate career at a luxury hotel company felt crushing. Being an executive on the Senior Leadership team felt like a trap. My heart was confined in this little box. My obsession with perfection was exhausting.

At the time, I blamed it all on my boss. He had pretty high standards. He shared with me once that racehorses were meant to be ridden, implying I was that horse. He cracked the whip, yet so many people said we were similar. But still, we clashed. I blamed him for smothering me and believed he had no interest in my ideas. When he was interested, he still added some sort of unattainable element that invited my failure—which I refused to let happen. It was the constant push to be better and better. My creations were never *good enough*.

Enter that tiny apple tree. And my dad. With time and support I finally connected the dots. I was feeling this way about my boss because of unfinished business with my father. In my mind, I believed that to win my boss's approval, I had to be perfect all of the time, which was *exactly* how I felt while growing up around my father. There was no admiration or affection or acknowledgement from my boss or my father unless I was killing myself to accomplish some feat that seemed impossible. When I achieved the impossible, then I was the "good girl." Then I received the attention, the accolades.

I remember thinking it was more than just my boss. I felt like the company itself caused such discontent, driving its people into the ground to squeeze out every last possible drop of profit, regardless of how good the results were the year before. *Where does it end?* I would think. I felt like we were driven and driven and driven to the top, year after year after year. It was a total grind. Senior management was forced to make decisions that impacted line-level employees in negative ways, just so the company stock price could be maintained.

It was easy to admire my boss in these situations, as he fell on the sword, arguing that we should first eliminate the florals in the front lobby of the resort before having hourly employees have to pay for their own lunches. (one major benefit of working in a hotel.)

It was completely insane how they pushed me and everyone else year after year. Didn't they know how hard we worked? Didn't they realize we received three hundred emails every single day and that it was impossible to get it all done? Didn't they know that there was barely time to go to the bathroom, let alone eat lunch?

A twelve-hour day, which hardly made a dent in the workload, left me feeling depleted, disgusted and directionless. Any sense of accomplishment or completion was short-lived.

But I loved the paycheck and the epic beachside location, so I pushed down the frustration and exhaustion. I was making a lot of money and working at a beautiful place. I liked the people

I worked with. They were good, caring people. They were the best in class. They had to be, as my boss only kept the very best.

Was I bored of the monotony? Twenty-eight years of being there every day. Twenty-eight annual budgets. Twenty-eight times imagining a grand plan for the year ahead, only to have the corporate office come through with its machetes, butchering all of the fun, innovative plans we imagined carrying out. As much as I wanted to blame my boss, he received the brunt of it all, getting crap from the owner and senior leadership.

I had been to the dance so many times before that it didn't matter if it was this company or a different one. They all had the same MO: Profit, Profit, Profit! At any cost. Or at least that's how it felt.

Listen, I took this job at the leading luxury hotel company because it looked *really* good on paper. Beautiful, successful, prestigious, world-class resort fifteen minutes from my house. Check. A seat on the executive team, making a great base salary, and the potential for really big yearly bonuses. Check. The promise of stepping away from the sales effort and fully immersing myself in the marketing aspect, which I truly did love. Check. But now it was really clear: For me, this was a soul-crushing environment, and inside I was dying.

And here's the thing: *All of this drama was really just going on in my own mind.* With the help of experienced coaches and some deep inner work, I realized I was the one who was 100 percent responsible for the experience I was having, but I refused to see or accept that responsibility at the time. The truth was that my boss was a brilliant visionary who was asking for the best from his people. It was just easy to make him my scapegoat. The truth was that I *knew* I didn't want to work at a hotel anymore. It was no longer a fit for me. Maybe it never was. Maybe I forced myself into this position, which I excelled at for many years, because I thought I should. Even in my previous job—I was the West Coast VP of sales and marketing—I had a lot more freedom and control, yet deep down I was still deeply unfulfilled. Deep down, I knew that I wasn't happy and that I needed more. But I just wouldn't look.

I took the job for reasons that would satisfy my ego: safety, security, comfort, and control. I stayed with the job because at the time, there was not one bone in my body that believed that I was talented enough, capable enough, or smart enough—or that I had enough time—to start a brand-new career in something else. I also had zero aspiration to pursue any other career. I had spent twenty-eight years climbing the ladder, and I wasn't willing to give up my perceived status or salary level. Doing anything else wasn't even a possibility for me. I stayed becoming more miserable by the day.

Thank God my Higher Self stepped in. It knew what it was doing, even if I didn't. My mother always said I was impulsive, but now, knowing myself and my patterns well, I believe this impulsiveness was my Higher Self leading me. My intuition. In a way, I had to trick my logical mind into doing something new. If my logical mind got too involved, it would surely sabotage my dreams.

So, why was I so miserable?

As it turns out, that's what happens. It's built into "the plan". A divine plan, more vast than retirement packages and annual bonuses. If someone doesn't change and grow for positive reasons, life will become intolerable.

I was miserable because I needed to remove myself from that situation—at any cost. I needed to peel back the layers in order to uncover my true desires. I needed to discover what would bring me a deep level of fulfillment and purpose. I wanted to feel like I was making a difference in life.

American author Joseph Campbell describes the hero's journey as this: "A hero ventures forth from the world of common day into a region of supernatural wonder: fabulous forces are there encountered, and a decisive victory is won: the hero comes back from this mysterious adventure with the power to bestow boons (prizes, things or new ways that are beneficial for) ... his fellow man."

Well, this is certainly what happened to me.

In the summer of 2013, desperate for answers in my life, I went to see a psychic. I cried to her (as I had done to many intuitives before), saying, "Help me find my purpose. I must find my purpose."

She said, "Donna, your guides are spelling it out for me: S-P-I-R-I-T-U-A-L P-S-Y-C-H-O-L-O-G-Y."

I said, "What the hell is Spiritual Psychology?"

She said that there were three universities that taught a program in this field. Two were in Northern California: Sophia University and the California Institute for Integral Studies, but she never gave me the name of the third one because we got distracted while talking about something else. I went home from the psychic reading filled with curiosity about Spiritual Psychology, so I consulted the other oracle: Google. The third university was the University of Santa Monica.

The program at the University of Santa Monica took place once a month for ten months. It was pricey but doable. And

Santa Monica was less than two hours north of where I lived in Orange County.

After a long back-and-forth with an admissions counselor named Veronica Alweiss, to whom I am eternally grateful, I worked through my ego's 101 logical arguments for why *not* to do this. And then, finally, after months of discussion, I enrolled.

The master's program at the University of Santa Monica changed my life in every way possible. This exquisite, personal, experiential journey into myself—designed by co-directors, president, chief academic officer, and the master spiritual teachers Drs. Ron and Mary Hulnick—quite literally transformed me from the inside out. This elegant and impeccable container of safety and love gently ushered me into being *me* at the deepest level. It was the catalyst that pushed me to reveal myself not only to *myself* but also to the rest of the world.

As I found my voice, I realized I have a song to sing. This is a song I have loved for a long time: the song of Spirit. USM invited me to sing it with clarity and grace. Now I want to fly to the top of the mountain and sing it at the top of my lungs. And I've discovered, I want to do that for *me*. Because I have something deep inside me that *must* sing this song. If someone hears my song, likes it, and wants to sing along, that is wonderful. And if not, that is totally fine, too.

Today, I am a Soul-centered catalyst for others' personal transformations. I serve in the roles of transformation consultant, spiritual mentor, and professional life and business coach. In the grand scheme of it all, I am young in this profession. I started leading personal coaching journeys, teaching master classes, and facilitating Soul-centered workshops in 2014. I successfully walked away from my old life as a marketing executive, left the corporate arena, and transformed my entire human adventure by starting in a totally new profession in the middle of my life. I've found the meaning and purpose I was seeking, and I'm earning a six-figure salary while making a meaningful contribution to the world doing something I love. And, I'm here to show you how.

I've served hundreds of clients across the globe, and they have experienced positive results in their lives within the physical world. For example, Tina raised her income by 20 percent, Lisa wrote and published her first book, and Jolene found the courage and the tenacity to launch her first album. But most importantly, these women (and my other clients, too) have experienced profound shifts in their inner worlds. They've found more peace, calmness, inspiration, clarity, and confidence. And they now consistently and more fully integrate their Soul essence where it really matters in their lives. This is what I learned to do, as well.

The Purpose of This Book: Personal Transformation

The unique framework of this book is my personal transformation from living a Soul-depleting, effortful life "of doing" to living a joy-filled, affirming, in-the-flow, graceful life of "Being."

I have combined my miraculous true stories with life-changing teachings. I've also included Opportunities for Transformation, which are actionable exercises, and Sacred Truth Activations, which are personal decrees to reclaim one's authentic empowerment.

I have blended my 50+ years of life adventures with my 35+ years of immersing myself in spiritual materials, study, and awareness, and I have included what I have learned from my teachers in the classroom at USM as well as what I have learned from the inner sanctuary of my interior world. Let me be completely honest and say that the learnings I present here are my own distillation and understanding of what I was taught by the many masters upon whose shoulders I stand. It is my honor and privilege to be the curator of these ideas. My viewpoint is just my expression. That said, I believe there are two key aspects that make this book unique:

The first is that I have included real-life stories about the miracles and grace that have unfolded in my life. My besties and I say, "You can't make this shit up." And you can't. Through this incredible unfolding, my intention is to make some important connections for you along the way. For me, connecting these dots evolved in a slow and organic way. I married this knowledge with the wisdom I've gained from my life adventures. Sewing all of this together, I experienced epiphanies and an awareness that made my Spirit soar and remember the truth of who I am deep in the core of my Being. My clear intention is to share my life and my learnings in a way that inspires you to take action and integrate these ideas into your own life.

I could not have organized or articulated these ideas had it not been for my education at the University of Santa Monica. Beyond just cognitive understanding, the transformation I had the privilege of experiencing at USM is integrated within me not only intellectually but also as a spiritual awakening throughout my whole Being. As a result of what took place throughout this journey, I have experienced an entire metamorphosis that has, similar to the change from a caterpillar to a butterfly, reordered all of me from the inside out. Without that transformation, I would not have had the courage to step out of my secure comfort zone and old patterns of familiarity in order to live in what Drs. Ron and Mary Hulnick term as "the Divine Unknowing."

I have been a spiritual seeker since the young age of five. I have read hundreds of books and am deeply grateful for the wisdom and knowledge that has been shared by so many. Ron and Mary take it to a different level. They have created a sacred container and guided processes that invite us out of the conceptual idea of Spirit and into the experiential knowing of the truth of our Beingness and who we really are as Spiritual Beings having human experiences.

Perhaps the most important aspect of this material is the opportunity it gives you to take action and integrate what you are reading into your life. The only way real transformation can occur is by engaging with life. You have to test things out. To be willing to get out of your comfort zone, take a risk, and experience the rewards that are derived from that leap.

I include a call to action in each chapter, or what I call an "Opportunity for Transformation." These self-guided activities are for engagement. They are presented in the form of personal reflections, journal prompts, and downloadable worksheets, where you can personally engage yourself and take action for the purpose of experientially understanding what you just learned. I took lots of action, which you will read about, and that is one of the key factors that now makes me qualified to share this wisdom with you.

The personal decrees I include, found at the end of each chapter, are called "Sacred Truth Activations." They serve as a healing transmission and are acts of self-love that are presented in the first person. They are invitations for you to reclaim your personal power, and they are meant to be read aloud. When you speak them into the Universe, you will experience rich embodiment and ownership of the lessons being imparted. To deepen the experience of the OFT exercises and the STA transmissions, you can also access downloadable versions at DonnaBond. com/OpportunityforTransformation and DonnaBond.com/ SacredTruthActivations.

To that end, within these pages are sacred truths, universal law, and spiritual concepts. I consider all of it to be your Original Wisdom. That's right, all of this is already part of *your* Original Wisdom. You're just using me and this book to remember what you already know. Engaging with this material can assist you in waking up, shifting your perception, changing your life, and transforming your consciousness. I invite you to weave it all together, in the order in which it is presented. I invite you into a new level of awareness as you integrate these sacred truths into your life and your consciousness. Through it, you harness the power of your Original Wisdom.

As each chapter unfolds, you can amass these lessons and use them as life-mastery tools that can be incorporated into your journey going forward. Each chapter ultimately imparts a mindset shift, allowing you to determine how this new perspective can support you in your life's expansion. This book is a journey of self-discovery. I invite you to give yourself permission to examine rules you live by that may no longer be serving you.

I'm most serious about doing the activites throughout the book. It was the brilliant master coach Steve Chandler who outlined the distinction between *information* and *transformation*. A lot of us take in information through books, lectures, workshops, and so on. Trust me, I know this because I am a book glutton, and I've attended *a lot* of workshops about these topics. And here's the thing: That information didn't change the experience of my life. Transformation, however, can only occur by taking action. It requires interaction and engagement with life. Transformation requires feedback from the Universe. Transformation comes through failure and triumph, it requires personal revelation, and it is informed by responses from the world around you and the world within you. Only by taking action are you truly able to transform.

What Will You Get from This Book?

I want to inspire you to know you are greater than anything you can imagine. To know that you are made from the same creative power as the universe. My intention is to reflect the profound truth of who you really are and to ignite the brilliant Light within you. This book is the framework you can use to harness the power of your Original Wisdom. You are invited to stop hiding. Nothing is more important at this time on the planet than the reclamation and the expression of the authentic *you*. What is inside of you is the foundation to a rich, miraculous, and fulfilling life. With this book, you will:

- Recognize, respect, and honor your sweet self so you can experience your wholeness.
- Celebrate your Human Self with reverence and trust your Higher Self with confidence.
- Learn to embrace everything on your path, so you can continue to grow.
- Embody a new way of being, to invite personal evolution into your life.

- Observe the miracles in your ordinary daily life so you can enrich your experience.

- Let go of old identities and stories of not enoughness and reclaim your authentic self.

- Identify new beliefs to consider and cultivate supportive behaviors to adopt.

- Develop a practice of radical self-acceptance to stop the *"doing"* and embrace a new *"Way of Being"*.

- Transcend fear and courageously take action.

- Develop self-trust and listen to your intuition.

- Raise your personal vibration to clarity your life's purpose.

I'm sharing my story with you in the hopes that it will resonate inside you at a deep level and inspire you to wake up and reclaim your sovereignty as a divine Being who is having a human adventure. Deep within you, you know all of this because it's your Original Wisdom. I am just here to ignite it.

Original Wisdom is
What is True Within You

You are a divine, spiritual Being on a human adventure. The divine part of you is made of the energy of Love. The purpose of your life is the expression of that energy of Love and all that is encoded within. Your life's experiences are seeded through your thoughts and beliefs. Your intuition is the lifeline between your Higher Self and your Human Self. Harnessing your power of creation occurs by taking responsibility for your "I AM" presence. The key to loving your sweet self is the radical acceptance of your wholeness. Original Wisdom is the inherent intelligence in all of us that is rooted in unconditional Love.

In 2012, I turned forty-four. This is when the seed in me began to reawaken. Forty-four was how old my father was when he died. This sobering reality was the wake-up call I needed in order to realize I might not have much time left on this planet. This was when I began to get serious about asking the questions like "Who am I?" and "Why am I here?" and "What is life about?" It was through these inquiries that I discovered my own Original Wisdom. Through that discovery, I experienced a reclamation of authentic power, a profound sense of inner freedom, the knowing that I am the presence of Love, and the recognition of my own divine essence. My intention is to pass the torch to you.

There is a story of a mythical lost land called Avalon, which the ancients believed existed in a different realm, enveloping "All That Is." Avalon literally means "The Isle of Apples." The magical unfolding of this initiate's story leads us on a winding path right into the mystical and indelible Isle of Apples. There are many legends about this sacred land, and they revere King Arthur, the Holy Grail, goddesses, high priestesses, and the magical healing grounds themselves. The initiate once heard that legends and myths are really about how our own true stories are interwoven within our lives.

The apple is a symbol of fertility, love, joyousness, wisdom, and divination, and it represents totality and unity. Avalon is the place where two worlds converge. Our initiate unknowingly followed the trail of the apple, which led her squarely and blindly across a bridge magically connecting those two worlds—those being the "real world" (physical) and the "other world" (spiritual). She had always had a sense that there was more, a power *within. When she heard the call from her Soul, which was urging her to seek this "something more," she was unaware at the time that she was being led directly into this magical lost land.*

The mist-enshrouded apple island of ancient magic and myth is an entrance to the world of Spirit. Here, one experiences his or her infinite nature. It is also a place where—through the nurturance of Mother Earth, the sovereignty of the Divine Feminine, and your inherent Original Wisdom—we learn to fully embrace the wholeness of our humanness and our spiritual nature. In our modern world, The Isle of Avalon is hidden behind the veil that is located in the physical place we know today as Glastonbury, England. Perhaps the spiritual world is a lot closer than we think.

Chapter One

The Power Within

"I cannot tell you any Spiritual truth that deep within you don't know already. All I can do is remind you of what you have forgotten."

~ Eckhart Tolle

Manifesting My Apple – My Personal Awakening

Six months into the master's program at USM, in March of 2014, my husband and I were experimenting with exercises in creating our own reality, based on Pam Grout's book *E-Squared,* which offers nine do-it-yourself experiments. One particular exercise focused on asking the Universe for assistance in manifesting a specific object. I asked the Universe to bring me an apple (an apple was simple, random, and lacked emotional charge). At the time, apples meant nothing to me. I don't remember even being particularly fond of apples, so it was unlikely that anyone would offer one to me. Nor did I consciously remember my dad mowing down my apple tree at that time. It seemed like a fun experiment to manifest something so random. But little did I know, I was tapping into the energy of the quantum field! I set my clear intention one Sunday evening while my husband and I were in bed, about to fall sleep. I said out loud, in a summons, "Universe, bring me an apple this week!"

The next morning, I left town on an airplane, headed to my company's Global Exchange Conference in Dallas. This meeting would lay out the company's strategic direction for the new year, and it also included the annual award ceremony for the previous year's accomplishments. It was a major opportunity for networking with peers.

I had just earned a large bonus check and had also received a glowing annual review from my boss. For the most part, I was feeling good about my job. On some level, however, I knew this temporary glimmer was unsustainable, because deep down I had been covering up my misery ever since I'd started the position. I was getting good at stifling my feelings and ignoring my unhappiness.

If I'm honest, my dissatisfaction had started long before, when I was a VP of sales and marketing at another company. I lost my job, along with sixty other people, when the company closed its doors in 2010. Truly, I had been feeling dejection and depression since then. But in my new position, my ego was feeling valued and recognized, and it was easy to look at all of the incredible material things my profession afforded me. I masked my true self—my feminine, spiritual, ancient, original wisdom-knowing, high-priestess self, which believed in magic and miracles—and kept on keeping on.

Behaving like a buttoned-up, emotionless corporate executive was not good for my health. My body was in numbing discomfort most of the time. I settled into my window seat on the plane and suddenly became aware of the acute pain in my shoulder and my right arm. This pain had persisted for almost nine months. That day, the inflammation felt visible, and my nerves were literally screaming. The agony made me tired and emotional, so I applied the strategy that works wonders for corporate executives worldwide: I ignored it.

I burrowed up against the window to read Ken Robinson's *Finding Your Element*. The book was assigned reading for my master's program at the University of Santa Monica. I had high hopes for this book because, for my entire life, I'd been on a quest to find my element, and I thought this book would help. Before my career began, I thought, as many of us do, that life was about pursuing money and material things. As my career progressed and I attained these things, I thought the next step was to find love. Once I found love, my health started going downhill because I was unknowingly suppressing the expression that wanted to be set free in the world. What was going to make me happy? Was that even possible? I found myself nearing the last pages of Robinson's book, no closer to finding my element than when I had started. As I read, my body began "speaking louder." My shoulder was throbbing and visibly swollen.

Trying to ignore the pain, I read, "Navigating your life is like being on the open seas. You can cling close to the known shores or you can set a more exploratory course." I read on. "Mark Twain used this same metaphor in his famous quote: 'Twenty years from now you will be more disappointed by the things you didn't do than by the ones you did do. So, throw off the bowlines. Sail away from the safe harbor. Catch the trade winds in your sails. Explore. Dream. Discover.'" My mind raced about the concept of playing it safe. Issues I hadn't been willing to look at suddenly bubbled up. Thoughts echoed like a chorus: *You're gonna be more disappointed by the things you didn't do.*

Robinson continued with another quote from Ralph Waldo Emerson: "'What lies behind us and what lies before us are tiny matters compared to what lies within us.'" I felt pressure in my ears, and it was moving up into my head. Thoughts I had been trying to push down were like a pile of bricks on my chest. Robinson shared that "finding your element is about discovering what lies within you and in doing so, transforming what lies before you."

What lies within me? I began to wonder, and I felt a deep knowing that there was something more in me rising to the surface. And then the tears came as I read the clincher, a tiny eight-line poem by Elizabeth Appel (not Anaise Nin, as I once thought) that would become the catalyst for the profound life changes I would go on to make. The poem made my heart and my head burst open. It connected so poetically to the metaphor of my frozen shoulder.

Risk
And then the day came,
When the risk
To remain tight
In a bud
Was more painful
Than the risk
It took
To blossom.

I abruptly became conscious of the sobs. With tears flowing down my face, I brought my knees to my chest, hoping no one on the plane would notice. After a crystal-clear dose of divine guidance and pure inner knowing, I suddenly understood that the pain in my shoulder and the fact that I couldn't lift my arm above my chest were my Soul's ways of getting my attention. I knew with complete clarity that this intense physical experience was directly connected to my suppressing my own potential. In that moment, the poem illustrated to me, loud and clear, that I was remaining tight in the bud.

All at once, it no longer mattered that I didn't have "a plan" or that I had yet to "find my element." *Shit!* I thought, *I'm forty-four years old. This is the age dad was when he died.* I knew that it was time to stop complaining, to stop with the excuses, and to quit this job that I did not love. I needed to decide how I wanted to spend the rest of the fleeting time I had left on the planet. I needed to stop playing it safe, or I might die. I knew with all of my true inner knowingness that I had to embark on a journey of reinvention. It didn't matter what people thought or what they would say when I walked away from the money, the recognition, and what many thought was one of the best jobs in the world. I somehow knew it was going to be okay, and I just sat there and cried. I cried because of the pain, and I cried because of the truth I had just discovered inside of me. I cried in awe, and I cried in gratitude. I cried from embarrassment, and I cried from shame, and I cried because of the rawness of the realization that "all this" was not "all that." And mostly, I cried in relief because finally, after so many years of pretending, I was admitting to myself that it was up to me to make a change.

I got through the company event because I *knew* it would be my last conference. I moved through the program, but now I was looking through a different lens. Usually, I was the first one

to the break-out room. I would grab a seat in the front row, take
copious notes, and plan how I would implement all of the new
ideas when I returned to the office. None of this happened. I was
quiet, reserved, and kept to myself. I felt pride for this organization and for my twenty-eight-year career in hospitality. For a
girl like me—an average, middle-class ladder-climber—I knew I
had done okay. Sure, it was time for a change—a BIG change—
but attending this conference was like a grand crescendo to my
entire career. Sorta like a farewell tour. I found myself expressing
gratitude for the adventure so far.

On the last night, I enjoyed a wonderful dinner in typical
luxury-hotel style, with all the beauty and elegance of a first-
class meal in a magical setting. I had a lovely time, secure in my
inner knowing that this was the last dinner of this kind that I'd
be having for a while. I had emotionally embraced my decision
to move on and, as a result, was able to relax and be myself,
not really giving a damn about what anyone thought about
who I was or what I said. The gentleman sitting next to me was
showing us pictures of the titanium in his leg. He was recovering
from a terrible motorcycle accident. I talked about energy medicine and holistic healing with my dinner companions, sharing
my new sense of personal freedom. I felt amazing expressing
thoughts and ideas I had loved while I was a student of metaphysics. I was letting Spirit Girl out of the closet, and it felt
so good.

Without feeling shy in any way, I told my tablemates, "This is
way more fun and interesting than talking about sales and marketing!" We all laughed.

My name was called through the microphone on stage. For the
third year in a row, I was the recipient of the Western Regional

Marketing Achievement Award. Three times the charm. For almost three decades, I had worked my way up the corporate ladder in hospitality. I had been incredibly driven, dropping everyone and everything for the next best job. I had walked away from friends, community, and even my first husband. Time and time again, I chose my career. I was now at "the top," and I also knew this chapter of my life was complete. I was eager to move forward on the path of self-discovery and find my element. I had absolutely no clue what that looked like, how it was going to happen, or how I would support myself, and I knew I would figure it out. For the first time in almost a decade, I felt crystal clear.

As I walked back to my dinner table, clutching my award, I saw that dessert was being served. I gazed down at the elegant final course. It looked good. I didn't realize what was happening until I read the menu card: apple composition, almond clafoutis, and apple confit with green apple sorbet. My jaw fell open. I thought, *Are you f-ing kidding me?* I glanced up and looked around. *Oh my God*, I thought, *there is no one here who will get this story.* No one in the room would understand why I had been trying to manifest an apple. I had kept this part of myself hidden because I was pretty sure people would think I was nuts. I kept Spirit Girl locked in the closet, where she'd been since my early twenties. No one in my corporate world knew she was part of me.

Spirit Girl is the real me. The true me. The part of me who loves spirituality and metaphysics and psychology. She's the girl who went to psychics and had her astrology read and who devoured every metaphysical, spiritual, and self-help book she could find. She is the girl who is the modern-day mystic hiding in a closet. She's the girl who enrolled herself in a master's program in Spiritual Psychology, on top of working sixty hours a week. She is the high priestess who came here to teach that there are many different pathways to God.

I sat in awe, marveling that the Universe and the powers within it had allowed me to create my own reality. Marveling at the power that was part of me. I sat, dazed at the timing, which could only be considered a miracle! I was astonished, shocked, and humbled to receive this direct nod from the Universe itself, congratulating me on a job well done, not for winning the damn award, but for finally realizing my truth within. I smiled, knowing I was ready to reinvent myself and knowing that I had the support of the gods. Tears stung my eyes, and love opened my heart as I acknowledged the profound power of the moment. My life experience thus far had bestowed many gifts upon me, and I was grateful for each and every one of them.

I looked down at my apple dessert, a deep knowing in my heart. *I am a Spiritual Being having a human adventure. I am a unique, individualized expression of the Divine. I just freaking manifested an elaborate display of apples.* And in that moment, I knew I was far more powerful than what I had previously thought I was, and I suddenly had a deep understanding of the possibilities within me and within the world.

Have you ever had the sense that you are so much more than what you thought you were?

The Universal Life Force

To help you understand the magnificent vastness of you, let's start here. There is an Infinite Intelligence powering the Universe. Let's call it the Life Force. This Life Force is breathing life into you. In spiritual terms, there is a whole other realm that you are part of and that you have within you, animating your physical body. This Life Force is greater than any situation you will ever encounter in your surroundings or in your environment. It keeps the planets in orbit and grows flowers and forests from simple seeds. It is the power shining our sun each morning and twinkling each star at night. The Life Force is the energy that powers every living thing on this planet. And you often completely overlook the fact that this is the same energy that also powers you.

At that company dinner—during dessert, of all things—I had come face to face with my own Life Force. The profound synchronicity of the apple reminded me of the magnificence of my *Beingness*. I share this with you to remind you of yours. I am reminded of the David Dellinger quote about miracles: "There are only two ways to live your life. One is as though nothing is a miracle. The other is as though everything is a miracle." Isn't it so much better, and a lot more fun, when everything is a miracle? My hope is that as I unfold my many miracles for you, you will begin to look for miracles in your own life.

Which term for your Life Force resonates with you? Please know that I believe these terms are interchangeable, and you will find all of them throughout this book.

- Higher Intelligence
- Universe
- Spirit
- Essential Nature
- Soul
- Higher Self
- Source

- Infinite Intelligence
- One Mind
- Higher Mind
- Inner Entity
- Authentic Self
- Universal Energy
- Higher Power
- Original Wisdom
- Drop of God

Yes, God. I am adding God to the list because in this grand, omnipresent, infinite Universal Energy—of which we are all connected—you are a drop of God. In the same way that a drop of sea water is a part of and the same essence as the entire ocean. Every single living Being on this planet is a unique, individualized expression of the Divine.

The Essence of Your Spiritual Nature

My apple manifestation is about harnessing the power of my Original Wisdom and is the start of recreating my life and making it a declaration of that energy. Your spiritual form extends beyond your body and is part of this energetic system. Your spiritual form is your Soul, which is the connection between you and God as well as between you and the universal Life Force. As Infinite Intelligence, your Soul is the part of you that knows what is going on in your life, even when it seems like your ego (or your conscious mind) does not.

This is how I describe the difference between religion and spirituality. Religion is a specific set of organized beliefs and practices that are created with the intention of directing each member of the group toward what "the group" thinks God is. Spirituality is an individual practice that honors and acknowledges your energetic nature or multidimensionality. Spirituality is the practice of sensing the connection to something bigger than your personality or ego. And it typically involves a search for meaning in your life. That search is motivated by the desire for a sense of fulfillment, peace, and purpose.

Spirituality is about the relationship with your inner Beingness, and it is also your own personal and individual relationship with All That Is. In this awareness is the recognition—and really, the remembrance—of your own multidimensionality. You are first and foremost an energy system. Your wholeness essentially includes your spiritual Beingness. You are far greater than you have been giving yourself credit for up until now. And this book, and the thoughts and techniques of this book, have been written to guide you and, ideally, to give you the experience of this greater, multidimensional part of you.

You Are a Multidimensional Being Having a Human Adventure

We often think of ourselves as bodies and personalities with souls. Shifting your identity to that higher, infinite part of yourself can be an empowering step toward elevating your consciousness and awakening into the knowing that you are a divine, spiritual Being having a human adventure, not the other way around. Your Soul, the multidimensional aspect of your Being, is a spark of the Divine and is connected to All That Is.

Consider that your body and your personality are your Soul's avatar. In a video game, the avatar of a player is the digital person you see "running around" inside the video game. The person playing the video game uses this digital person inside the video game to accomplish challenges and quests. The avatar in a video game *allows* the person playing the video game to be *in* the game.

Now, let's see how this example can give us a better understanding of how our bodies, personalities, and Souls work together in the real world. An avatar is defined as an incarnation in human form. Your body and personality are your Soul's perfect disguise. Your body and personality *allow* your Soul to be *in* the world.

If you are living a life, you are on a spiritual path. It's simply a matter of the level of conscious awareness that you bring to your life and how you view the experiences unfolding around you. You can view the challenges and opportunities of your life as being perfectly orchestrated for your growth, learning, and expansion, or you can view them as irrelevant happenstance. This is your life, so you get to choose. (For me, the manifestation of an apple, in the form of a beautiful dessert, was a miracle bridging my multidimensionality and my humanness.)

We can refer to your Soul as your big "S" self. The big "S," being connected to All That Is, has a higher perspective on your life. This Infinite Intelligence holds the code that guides your experiences, ensuring that the lessons you came to this life to learn are unfolding for your highest good.. The big "S" can be considered the ultimate power source because of its limitless nature. The way you can imagine how this part of you gets down here to Earth is by picturing it as a concentrated point that is crystallized into your physical body. This energy, or Life Force, is what ultimately gives you life and is what makes you multidimensional.

Your small "s" self is your physical body and personality, which are primarily guided by the ego. The ego is connected to and concerned with the physical mind, and it operates logically in the physical world. The physical mind is almost like a computer database. This is the learned part of you, and it records all of the experiences you have had. This is where the ego and the personality go to check the mind's "data," meaning *past* experiences, to find a basis on which to determine a logical explanation to support future decision-making. In other words, the ego/personality can only make decisions for your future based on *the past*. It's important to recognize that even though you live in the physical world, there is an invisible, non-physical part of you that powers and animates your physical self.

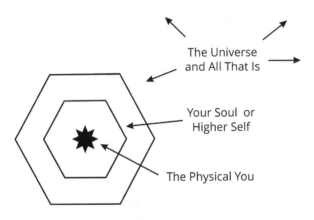

The Multidimensional You

The graphic above illustrates that this physical incarnation, your small "s" self, resides *within* the consciousness of your Soul, or big "S" self, and it also shows that your Soul resides within the consciousness of All That Is. The Soul and your physical self are just more narrowly focused projections of Higher Consciousness, allowing you to have more individual, specialized experiences in the physical world.

Imagine your Soul *chose* to have an incarnation, or "an assignment," here on Planet Earth, and it can only take place through the five senses that are embodied as the human adventure. Your Soul holds the map, helping you fulfill the assignment that is the lesson plan your Soul signed up to learn. Your Soul is the personal guidance system charting the course to the fullest expression of you in this life.

Acknowledging Your Inner Being

The incredibly wise, infinite part of your Being that is within you is guiding you all the time, yet many of us do not pay attention to this wisdom-filled part of our Beingness. Your Soul is pure energy, and it is very much alive and connected to *everything*. Developing a daily practice in which you acknowledge your Inner Being is a sacred ritual that can strengthen and sustain the relationship between the small "self" and the big "Self." Slowing down and recognizing this higher, authentic part of yourself each day builds confidence and trust in how your life is unfolding. You have my greatest encouragement to connect to and pay homage to this part of your Being. We will explore how to create a daily, self-honoring practice. You will see that making and keeping commitments to yourself is a sacred act of self-love.

Inner Knowing

Have you ever had an inner knowing that there is more to life but that you are unable to access what you're after? Have you ever had an experience in nature that invited you to "surrender to the beauty" of the moment? Have you ever just stretched out your arms, surrendered yourself to the Universe? Have you ever experienced energy rushing through you that allowed you to feel connected with love? If you have, you know what I mean. This book is all about integrating awareness of this higher part of yourself into your everyday human life.

My journey started with reading books and learning everything I could in order to unlock the secrets of the Universe. And what I really wanted was to unlock the secrets of myself. "Who am I, and why am I here?" My life's journey became about integrating the truth of my Authentic Self into my life. This process—the integration of my spiritual nature into my humanness—was always my purpose, but I didn't know it at the time.

The deep awareness I experienced on the airplane was a gift given to me by my Higher Self. This profound realization, along with the added encouragement from the Universe—in the form of an extravagant apple desert—was the kick in the ass my ego needed so that I could begin paying attention to the multidimensional aspect that is me. The same multidimensional aspect that is *you*.

In the next chapter, we will explore the cosmic glue that binds us all together. We are one family, one race, and one energy.

Opportunity for Transformation
Take Action

This is the first Opportunity for Transformation (OFT). This is your chance to take action and move your life forward, discover a new part of your consciousness, and create an experience for yourself that will deepen your learning of this material. All of the OFTs are designed to assist you in more fully integrating Original Wisdom from your Authentic Self into your day-to-day life. If you would like to download an actual worksheet or listen

to an audio version of this OFT, please visit donnabond.com/
opportunityfortransformation.

Being with Your Multidimensionality – Your Beingness

As with everything, my intention is to help you be more of you.
While I share these practices and invite you to give them a try,
I also want to encourage you to make them your own. Play
around with it. What feels right for *you*? Much of your life's
journey is about experimentation and the discovery of your own
flow and rhythm.

   The Process (You'll want to set aside ten minutes for this.)
First, get comfortable. I recommend you sit down as you experience this process. You won't want to be driving, as I'm inviting
you to go within. Close your eyes. Take a deep breath in through
your nose and release your breath through your mouth. Take a
few more breaths and simply notice the energy that is flowing in
and out of your physical body with ease. Focus your attention
on your heart space. Be quiet and be very still. Notice you have
the ability to observe your own thoughts. Observe them as if you
are watching a show. Do not become attached to these thoughts.
Do not judge them or get emotionally involved with them. Just
watch.

   Sit in the silence for at least five minutes (you can set a timer
to help you keep track of the time). Just sense the energy that is
running through you. Notice whether you can feel this energy
moving within you. This requires the utmost stillness.

   Now, acknowledge the "watcher," that place inside of you
that is the observer. This is your Higher Self, the big "S." In a
silent way, inside your mind, give a nod of reverence and gratitude to this part of your Being. Express your thanks for all of

the guidance given by this part of you and humbly ask that the guidance continue and become clearer throughout your life.

After you express your gratitude, and when you feel complete, slowly bring your awareness back to the room. Move your fingers, hands, and feet to come fully back into your body. Continue your day with refreshed energy and know that you are so much greater than what you may think.

Develop a Daily Practice

Your daily practice can be anything you want it to be, and it can be for any length of time. Some core elements to consider in a daily practice include:

1. Be aware that this time is time with *you*, for *you*, and about *you*. Connect with your Authentic Self, which is your higher wisdom and the reservoir of your energy source. This is how you make it clear to the Universe that *you* are important. By making and keeping this daily-practice commitment, in which you acknowledge your Human Self and your Higher Self every day, you let the Universe know you have put yourself at the top of your priority list.

2. Literally create a sacred space you can go to in order to be with yourself and your inner Beingness. This sacred space can be an entire room in your home or a small part of a room that you can use every day for your daily practice.

3. Allow this time to be devotional, like a ritual. Consider that you are honoring yourself as a divine Being and honoring the connection you have to All That Is as well as to your multidimensionality.

Get creative. Make it something you love. Perhaps find a patch of quiet carpet somewhere in your home. My space is on the floor in my bedroom, in front of a sliding glass door, where I can look out into my beautiful backyard and gardens. Perhaps in your space, you'll want to add "toys"—an array of treasures—such as crystals, essential oils, divinity cards, daily affirmations (see chapter "I AM"), poetry, *A Course in Miracles*, a dream journal, a writing journal, and figurines of Buddha and goddesses. Whatever feels nurturing and sacred to you.

My practice has a core element of twenty-five minutes of silent meditation, and then I "play" with the sacred jewels that occupy my space. What I play with depends on what I am called to receive in the moment.

If you take away one concept from this book, let it be the one that supports you in beginning a daily practice of honoring your sweet self. My practice, as you will read in chapter seven, quite literally saved my life.

Sacred Truth Activation

This is the first Sacred Truth Activation, and it is meant to be read out loud. You may experience the remembrance, awakening, and igniting of your Original Wisdom. You may feel a bit awkward the first few times you read this. That's okay. Some people may experience a little bit of a challenge while attempting to acknowledge how magnificent they are. That's okay. Each of this book's Sacred Truth Activations will assist you in integrating more of your Soul Essence, your multidimensionality harnessing the power within. You may wish to find a quiet, private space to speak these words aloud. Perhaps light a candle and spend a minute centering yourself before you begin. If you would like to listen to an audio version of this guided personal decree, please visit donnabond.com/sacredtruthactivations.

I Am a Multidimensional Being

I am a magnificent, unique, individualized expression of the Divine. I am an infinite, limitless, multidimensional Being. The energy that I am comprised of is the same energy of All That Is. The purpose of my life and spiritual journey is to awaken my inner knowingness and to recognize who I really am, which is the energy of pure, divine Love. Walking the spiritual path is a sacred act of remembering that I am a divine Being having a human adventure. In the journey of my life, I am here to authentically embody the power within. The majesty of the brilliant energy system that is me is so much more than I can even imagine in my human form.

With these words, I claim the authentic power of my Soul's magnificence and begin to see my life through the eyes of the creator I am. I know that by my mere existence I am worthy beyond measure, and I am enough. I am Love itself.

As a divine Being, the essence that is powering my human body is an energy system. This energy system is part of and connected to the larger, universal Life Force that is Source energy. I am divinely connected to and part of that great source, and in that I can relax, knowing I have a senior partner—my Higher Self, my big "S,"—which is guiding me, loving me, protecting me, and nudging me.

My Soul—my spiritual nature, my Inner Being, my multidimensionality—is highly motivated to learn the life lessons I choose to learn and to see the adventure of being human as loving. I allow myself to be in the silence and to recognize the divine, loving essence that I am. I feel ease and effortlessness in my expression of life. My Soul is highly energized. This energy that is me is the energy of inspiration and love. It is always with me, always available to me. It is the essence of the truth of who I am. It is my Authentic Self. It is my authentic power within.

The Isle of Avalon is a cosmic power point on the planet. This physical location represents the energetic portal of the frequency of love. It resonates with the energy of the Heart Chakra of our Mother Earth. *This energy we understand as love. It also happens to be the same energetic vibration that is the truth of each one's Beingness. This energy is weaving our initiate in with everyone else in this cosmic tapestry called life. This energy is the great mystery itself, and it is guiding her, inviting her, accepting her, loving her, and healing the shattered fragments through a sacred process of uniting in Oneness. To the goddess, this metamorphosis is the sacred grandeur that is actualized along the path to Avalon. The realization of this is her Original Wisdom. This divine gift is her eternal companion. Our initiate can only be granted this revelation and embodiment of the goddess by answering the call.*

Chapter Two

Everything Is Energy

"If you wish to understand the Universe,
think of energy, frequency and vibration."

~ Nikola Tesla

In Deepak Chopra's book *The Spontaneous Fulfillment of Desire*, he states that when the Universe is trying to get your attention, and when you are on the right track, it will be revealed to you through serendipity and grace. When these types of "coincidences" occur, you have a choice: You can treat them like everyday occurrences, or you can treat them like miracles.

We Are One Energy

To gain a better understanding of the role you play in the overall scheme of the Life Force, it's crucial to understand energy. For people who are triggered by the idea of God, or who just don't believe in God, I invite you to believe in energy, which is essentially the Infinite Intelligence powering the Universe.

Science informs us that everything is made up of energy. EVERYTHING. It is the foundation of all matter, which is made

up of particles. The energy that composes your body and your
consciousness is the same energy that composes the bricks of the
house you live in, your car, your phone, animals, trees, and your
thoughts. Energy vibrates at different levels to make it appear
as if there are separate objects. But it's all the same substance.
Einstein proved energy is everywhere and is neither created nor
destroyed; it is merely expressed in different forms and shapes.
It is constantly in motion and is changing form all the time. The
same molecules that make up a distant star may now be part
of your body. You may be breathing the same atoms that were
breathed by Buddha.

Without our connection to this Life-Force energy, our hearts
would not beat and breath would not flow through our lungs.
It is this energy that gives us LIFE. And it is this energy that
powers our physical bodies. This is the same energy that powers
nature and that keeps the planets spinning nicely around one
another so that they don't collide and cover us all in explosive
clouds of atomic dust.

So then, with this in mind, we are all part of *one* energy that
is simply expressed in different forms. We are collectively One
Universe and One Mind.

Dr. Joe Dispenza on the Energy of Quantum Physics

Dr. Joe Dispenza is an international lecturer, researcher, corporate consultant, author, and educator who studied biochemistry
at Rutgers University and who holds a B.S. degree with an
emphasis in neuroscience. I think Dr. Joe does a great job of artic-
ulating the close connection between science and spirituality.
I present it here for your consideration. If you're new to quantum
physics, I recommend that you just let these words wash over

you. Remember, we are all energy, and we are all connected. This means there is a part of each of us that understands what Dr. Joe is saying, even if we don't.

In his book *Breaking the Habit of Being Yourself,* he says, "Mind and matter are completely entangled. Your consciousness (mind) has effects on energy (matter) because your consciousness is energy and energy has consciousness. In the quantum model, the physical universe is an immaterial, interconnected, unified field of information, potentially everything but physically no thing. The quantum universe is just waiting for a conscious observer (you or me) to come along and influence energy in the form of potential matter by using the mind and consciousness (which are themselves energy) to make waves of energetic probabilities coalesce into physical matter. Just as the wave of possibility of the electron manifests as a particle within a specific momentary event, we as observers cause a particle or groups of particles to manifest physical experiences in the form of events in our lives."

Dr. Joe continues. "Humans and the quantum field are interconnected through the concept of quantum entanglement. Once two particles can be initially linked in some way they will always be bonded together by space and time. As a result, anything that is done to one is done to the other. This means that since we too are made up of particles, we are all implicitly connected beyond space and time. What we do unto others, we do unto ourselves. Is this a game changer or what?"

Everything Has a Frequency

According to Esther Hicks (often credited as Abraham), an American inspirational speaker and author, "You are creating by virtue of what you are thinking about, so there is no advantage whatsoever of pondering, remembering, observing or speaking of things you do not want. Make your active vibration be about what you do want and notice how quickly your life changes to match your vibration."

If everything is energy, then so are our thoughts. It began to be apparent in my life that my thoughts were how I communicated to the Universe what I wanted. Everything, including us, is always emitting or broadcasting a distinct energy pattern. And every energy vibration carries information. I realized the vibration of my thoughts attract and create my life. The Law of Conservation of Energy states, "Energy cannot be created or destroyed, it can only be changed from one form to another."

Because we are all one energy, each of us, as an individualized expression of the Divine, are the unique physical expression of that *one* essence. I sometimes imagine that our collective existence on Earth gathers data for God, like a giant computer that gains more and more intelligence from the data we collect and learn from. God knowing God. Could this be the purpose of existence? As humanity continues to evolve, part of what is occurring is that more and more of us are remembering we are connected to, and part of, God and each other. We are evolving still, but this time the evolution is not physical.

The evolution that is happening now is in our collective consciousness. The raising of our collective vibration (our country, our world) can only occur through the raising of our individual vibrations. Groups are just a bunch of individuals. The only way a group ever changes is when the individuals of that group change. When our vibrations are raised—when they go higher—we feel good. We remember we are energetic Beings of love.

Energy wants to expand. As we connect more and more to our authentic selves, our energies expand, and our vibrations naturally lift. Our Souls are always giving us clues about which direction to go by showing us what makes us *feel* more expansive and what makes us feel lighter. Conversely, if we're feeling contracted, we are making choices that are *not* allowing our Higher Selves to shine through.

Researchers found the vibratory frequency of emotions and learned through applied kinesiology and the acupuncture meridians that emotions resonate at various vibratory frequencies. The way I understand it, emotions of love, joy, and peace vibrate at a much higher level than emotions of shame, guilt, and hate. It makes sense then that when you are "swimming around" in the lower-frequency emotional states, you are hindering your own life and slowing down your growth. At the higher states, you feel expansive and can see life's possibilities.

The Law of Magnetic Attraction

The Law of Magnetic Attraction is always occurring and says that "like attracts like." This universal law is as real as the Law of Gravity. It stands to reason that if you are "swimming around" in lower-frequency emotions, that is the vibration you are resonating with and consumed in. This also means this "low vibration" is the signal you are broadcasting out. Consequently, the types of experiences you have are a vibrational match with this resonance. You invite more of the same into your life because that is how you are thinking and feeling.

Many of my clients, after clearing emotional debris and allowing themselves to reside in a higher vibratory frequency (such as willingness, acceptance, love, and joy), find that their lives keep getting better and better. For example, over the course of a few years, Olga began to shift her outlook on what she called "life's erratic behavior." Instead of seeing life as being against her and wrecking her plans, she began to open up to the possibility that she was being directed. This allowed her to move into willingness and acceptance. As she relaxed into life's events, now seeing them as helping her rather than hurting her, her entire outlook became more positive. This built upon itself, and today she texts me on a regular basis, sending messages that say things like, "I can't believe how much I love my life." As she lets go of trying to control things (which resulted in natural contraction), more of what she desires seems to naturally float into her experience.

When you experience the higher emotional states, your life becomes more positive. Because "like attracts like." You are literally pulling experiences to yourself. It's common sense to me that you feel better when you are experiencing emotions of joy and love rather than when you are experiencing emotions of fear and shame. What hasn't made sense to me until now is that the more time you spend "swimming around" in a particular emotion—or, in other words, at that particular vibratory frequency—the more you are inviting more of that same frequency (emotions and experiences) into your life.

The personal example I want to share is this: During the time of the global pandemic in June of 2020, I intentionally increased my meditation time, stayed away from the news, and consumed positive media and high-frequency music. (Just Google 528 HZ to experience high-frequency music.) As a result of maintaining a higher vibrational frequency in my own Beingness, my life seemed to unfold with harmony during this crazy time. I connected with and enrolled many new clients, abundance permeated my experience, and my husband and I spent our weekend afternoons lying around on the grass in the backyard, consumed with joy and love. We experienced life in synchronistic flow.

Feeling Good Is a Signal You Send Out

The thoughts and feelings you embody send out a signal to the Universe. All signals fulfill the spiritual Law of Attraction. Herein lies the value of raising your vibration. The mind's frequency is a magnet.

James Redfield is an American author, lecturer, screenwriter, and film producer. He is known for his novel *The Celestine Prophecy*. I believe it was James who first said, "Where your attention goes, energy flows." What you place your focus on energetically has a magnetic attraction to those things that you continue to place your focus on. *Your attention is energy*. Like attracts like. The universal Law of Attraction is always working. We are never taught about it, and it's invisible, so that is why most of us learn about this the hard way. You end up attracting and living what you don't want, because that is where your focus was. It works in tandem with your focus, and when your focus is on undesired things, those things—or the vibrational equivalent of them—are what then manifest themselves into your physical reality. And you don't realize you are creating them. You say things like, "That's just the way life is."

Some people will tell you this is BS. I make this claim because my life is living proof of this law, as are the lives of so many of my clients. I invite you to give it a try. Test it out. Don't take my word for it. Focus your attention on something that makes you feel good. Bring your attention to what brings you joy. Pay attention to how much of your energy you can focus in this way. If you are able to significantly shift your thinking to thoughts that bring you joy, you will begin to experience more joy. Test this out for yourself.

Are you radiating anger, upset, and conflict or love, peace, and harmony? The famous Beetles song "Good Vibrations" was named that for a reason. Feeling good is a signal you send out. You are naturally drawn to what makes you feel expanded, uplifted, alive, and joyful, because they are the resonance of the truth of your innate essence.

Energy Flows Where Attention Goes

Below is a chart depicting higher and lower vibrational words, attitudes, qualities, beliefs, and so on. Read into these with the higher, more energetic part of yourself. Notice how the higher-vibration words have a *feeling* of expansion and how the lower-vibration words have a *feeling* of contraction. Can you sense it?

Expansion	Contraction
Higher Vibration	Lower Vibration
Cooperation	Competition
Oneness	Separateness
Willingness	Resistance
Light-heartedness	Apathy
Courage	Hesitation
Joy	Anger
Peace	Disharmony
Love	Fear

Your emotions are the indicators that inform you whether what you are focusing on and thinking about is in or out of alignment with your Authentic Self. The multidimensional you is an energetic, vibratory frequency, and an intelligent one at that. When you are trying to do something and you experience lower-frequency energies, it's likely that you will feel constriction or contraction. Paying attention to this can provide you with important information. When you are following your joy, you are in a feeling of expansion. Your Authentic Self is always calling for you to expand. It's calling you to the higher frequency you are as the energy of Love.

There is a key difference between your underlying beliefs and how you are relating to something, especially when you consider the feeling of contraction. A feeling of contraction is often a feeling of resistance. This is a feeling of being closed down or stifled. This is an indication that you are out of alignment with your Authentic Self and are focusing your thoughts on something that you are not in acceptance of.

As you begin to pay attention to this always-present energy substance, of which you are a part, be aware and sense its expanded or contracted nature and use that intuitive intel as a compass that can assist you in directing your life. This same energy is the energy that connects us all, and it is the consciousness that is the fabric of our reality.

As an example, the United States of America (and a lot of the world) has shifted our awareness to "anti-racism." I want to suggest that it's important to shift our focus from the contractive keyword (racism) to what we do want to experience (unity, fairness, acceptance). Do you notice the shift in energy when you shift your focus from anti-racism to the term "race equality"? Do you feel an even more expansive sense of freedom and aliveness in the term "human equality"? The more we place our focus on the idea that race separates us, the more it does. I want to be very clear about the point I am intending to share here. As we continue to place our attention on racism, we energetically create an opportunity for more racism. Even when we put "anti" in front of it, we still have racism as the focus. And I really do understand that injustice needs to be front and center right now considering everything that has happened. I am just saying that if we want to truly move away from the things that divide us, we must place our energy, attention, and focus on how we can be united while celebrating our uniqueness.

Your Life Force – Invest Intentionally

One summer, half of my husband's lights blew out in his art booth at the Laguna Beach Festival of Arts. (He is an oil painter in the genre of magic realism. You can check him out at PaulBondart. com.) Within the span of thirty minutes, he fiddled with the lights, changed the bulbs, tinkered around, and even called the engineering department. But it seemed that no matter what he did, he couldn't get the lights to come back on and illuminate his art. Unlit art? No bueno.

I tried a little experiment with him. I said, "Let's focus on the lights that do work. Let's place our energy and attention on what we want." So, for about five minutes, we paid attention to the lights in the booth that did work. We totally shifted our focus off the lights that did not work. We admired the working lights, we felt gratitude for them, and we really recognized how beautiful they were making the art look. We completely shifted the focus of our energy off the lights that were not working and placed our attention (our energy, Life Force, energetic selves) on the lights that did. Literally, within five minutes, the other lights started working! We were full of excitement and enthusiasm. Even the engineering guy was stumped. He climbed down from his ladder, and shrugged his shoulders, and said, "I don't know." We were overjoyed by our little experiment. Coincidence, you say? No such thing in my world, and you can think what you want.

Opportunity for Transformation
Take Action

This is the second Opportunity for Transformation. This is your chance to take action and move your life forward, discover a new part of your consciousness, and create an experience for yourself that will deepen your learning of this material. All of the OFTs are designed to assist you in more fully integrating Original Wisdom from your Authentic Self into your day-to-day life. If you would like to download an actual worksheet or listen to an audio version of this OFT, please visit donnabond.com/opportunityfortransformation.

Expand and Contract Exercise

Sit for a few minutes and reflect over the last week. What happened? Where were you? Who did you meet or interact with? What were the experiences you had and the things you encountered? Now, take out your journal and a pen and make two columns. Label one of them "expand" and the other one "contract." Under the first column, list the things that occurred over the last week that made you feel expansive, and on the other side list the things that made you feel contractive. You can expand this exercise to encompass a month if this would be useful to you. The point of the exercise is to evaluate how you are spending your time and what you are giving your precious Life-Force energy to.

When you are experiencing things that cause you to expand, you are experiencing things that are "life giving." What are the things that make you feel good, that invoke feelings of growth, that invite feelings of happiness and joy? This exercise is meant to be a feeling exercise. Get out of your head and into your *body*. Be aware of these things and specifically feel the expansion or contraction.

When you experience things that cause you to contract, your Life-Force energy is being drained. When your Life Force is being depleted, you may experience emotional upset, and you can feel exhausted or even depressed.

After you've completed this exercise, evaluate your list. Consider the items that showed up on your expansion list and your contraction list. Are these things that you will likely repeat again next week or next month? Is that a positive thing? Consider whether these actions/behaviors/relationships are serving you and your life in the best possible way. Consider if this is how you want to be using your Life-Force energy.

In the expansion column, can you identify one or two things that really jump off the page? Is there something there that is trying to get your attention? Something that you love and that brings you joy and happiness? Something that you intend to allocate more of your time and attention to? Something that may have gone unnoticed until now? Maybe it's time to invest more time and energy in these things.

Sacred Truth Activation

This is the second Sacred Truth Activation. Find a quiet, private space to center yourself, light a candle, and speak these words aloud. If you would like to listen to an audio version of this guided personal decree, please visit donnabond.com/sacredtruthactivations.

I Am Energy

I am energy. I am made of the same material as the Earth and the stars. I am a unique, individual expression of energy, and no one else on this planet emanates the exact same energetic signature as I do. I am a drop of the Divine. I am connected to and part of the universal Life-Force energy. I am aware that I am the same essence as the Infinite Intelligence that powers the Universe. In that knowing, I am aware that I am a creator. I am learning that I am creating my experiences depending on where I place my attention. I am aware that where I place my attention is where I am commanding the molecules of the universal Life Force to go. My intention is to do this with loving for myself and for the highest good of all concerned.

I am the energetic frequency of pure, divine Love. When I am residing in a high vibrational frequency, I am aware of the presence of Love I am. I am also aware that I am able to shift out of a lower frequency by changing the direction of my thoughts. I am aware that as I align with the highest frequency of the Love that I am, I send this signal out into the world as a broadcast. I am broadcasting love. As I do this, I uplift others around me. As I reside in the energetic frequency of love,

I invite others to do the same. All I have to do to make this happen is be the presence of Love.

I understand that the direction of my attention is key in inviting the flow of energy in a particular direction. I am clear that, as a creator, I am creating the experiences in my life. I am kind and gentle with myself as I learn this. I am clear that situations, circumstances, and people in my life support the learning that I came here to experience. I am aware that the higher, energetic part of me is filled with my Original Wisdom, knowing, and guidance, and through my embodiment of the energy of Love that I am, I am able to more positively influence my own life.

It is only once she says yes to the journey of Avalon, with all its unlit passages and leaps of faith, that she is then shown the path. "The way" unfolds in real time. It is only by taking a step that the next one can be revealed. One must decide to walk through the field of infinite possibility. "The truth of the way" is shown only when she believes it's actually possible and only when she makes the choice to continue onward. It is the decision itself that swings open the gate, with gifts and blessings being yielded along the way.

Chapter Three

Choice Makes You a Creator

"It is in your moments of decision that your destiny is shaped."

~ Tony Robbins

The Universe prepared an elaborate and somewhat circuitous invitation that encouraged me to be a coach. To finish the Consciousness, Health, and Healing year of the master's program at USM, students were required to complete a project in which each person had to donate 66.5 hours "being of service." By the pool one afternoon at the Ojai Valley Inn and Spa, my girlfriends and I came up with a plan for my service: I would help individual, small-business solopreneurs with their marketing and provide coaching on how to be more confident. At this time, I wasn't a coach and knew nothing about coaching, but I figured I could help these new entrepreneurs envision their dreams, improve their self-confidence, and move toward achieving their goals. My girlfriend Nicola was particularly excited about this, and right then and there I agreed she would be the first person I would assist. Unbeknownst to me at the time, she also turned out to be my first client.

I followed through with "checking the box" and submitted my idea to the university. As much as this program was underscored by self-definition and discovery, there was no reason to think I wouldn't be able to follow through with my idea and fulfill the requirements for my service project in this way. My request, however, got denied. I didn't understand why. *What!* I thought. I had already made a six-month commitment to Nicola. *Where am I going to find all this extra time?*

While I was irritated that I now needed to come up with a new plan for a different service project, I upheld my sense of personal integrity and kept my promise. I coached Nicola for about nine months for free because I was "being of service." And it was magic. For her and for me. This was my first real understanding of what it means to get out of the way and allow Spirit to work through me. It was also my first understanding of true service. The gifts I received because of this "mistake" were extraordinary, mostly because I was discovering my work in the world—work that fulfilled me on multiple levels.

Many of the spiritual traditions and principles suggest that being of service is a quality of a high consciousness. I came from a "time is money" mentality. Growing up in the business world, it was unheard of to do anything unless one was getting paid for it. Today, I have a much different perspective about this. In my coaching practice, I offer a few complimentary coaching conversations each month. While this serves as part of my enrollment process, I coach a lot of people who will never go on an actual journey with me. This is part of how I "give back" in the world.

The important thing to acknowledge about this story with Nicola is that this was *not* my "plan." Even though I knew deep down that I had a desire to step out of the confined space of the corporate world, in no way did I foresee being a coach. I like to think the Universe saw an open door and helped fill in the blanks for me, and in a way I never could have imagined. In a way that was beautiful and magical and fulfilling on the deepest level. This was the first step I took toward being a coach, and I didn't even know it at the time. The Universe tricked me into it.

You Must Decide to Move Your Life Forward

In the scope of eternity, we are here on this planet for a nanosecond. Our lives are made up of a collection of moments. Those moments, when strung together, become time. Our lives are how we fill in those moments. And the experiences we have are comprised of the choices we make, and those choices propel our existence forward.

One really big choice you made that I invite you to reclaim is the decision your Soul made to take embodiment and come to this life. Yes, I know, this is SO HUGE! Just breathe. Here's the thing, it's incredibly difficult for our logical minds to make sense of this. In our linear thinking, we cannot understand the Soul's plan. We spend our lives trying to understand our own Soul-plan, so how could we try to understand someone else's? Yet, as difficult as this may be, see if *any* part of you feels the truth of this inside. If it does feel true, how does this change the view you have of your life? Do you feel more of a sense of empowerment? Can you accept that this grand adventure is unfolding for the benefit of your human evolution?

Every decision you make leads to the next and the next and the next and creates your life. If you do not make decisions for yourself, someone else may take the liberty of making them for you. When you believe that all of your decisions are being made for you, you feel disconnected from yourself and your choices, and this ultimately leads to feelings of depression and disempowerment. Can you sense how your energy expands when you take responsibility for making choices for yourself?

Each of us must choose for our individual selves. Consider reflecting on the idea that your Soul chose this lifetime, even with all its hardships and pain. Only you know what is true in your heart, though at times you may choose to ignore that inner knowing. When you make decisions for your life, you empower yourself simply by taking responsibility for your choices. The ability to make a choice is the act of taking a step forward, and it is a natural self-esteem builder and a cultivator of self-confidence and self-worth.

It's impossible to live a full, rich, happy, and fulfilled life without making decisions. If you desire change or want to move your life forward, you must make decisions. There is great power in the decisions you make for your life. (Even when they may not bring you exactly to the destination you have in mind. We'll address this in a minute.)

Various internet sources estimate that an adult makes about 35,000 decisions each day. Master Coach Mary Morrissey so brilliantly said, "What we trade our time for, we trade our life for." I say that the decisions we make along the way will greatly influence how we live and experience our lives.

Give Up the Guarantee

For most people, the reason they don't or won't make a decision in life is because they want a guarantee that what they decide is the "right" decision. This is governed by our good friend ego. Your ego wants to know that it's all going to work out in your favor. That you are not going to lose out on any time, money, relationships, and so on. The ego wants to know, with a high amount of certainty, all the steps from here to there, the return on the investment, and what the final and finished outcome will look like. The ego wants a guarantee that once you make a decision, it will all go your way. (Don't give the ego a bad rap. The truth is, you can't navigate physical reality without it.)

Oh, your beautiful little ego…that sweet, small self is trying to keep you safe and secure at every turn. Well, the truth is, this way of thinking is limiting and false. Remember, the ego likes to have past reference material on which to base its decisions. And when you are entering a landscape that is uncharted territory, the ego will discover it has no information on which to base its decisions. When you shine the light on this and acknowledge that this is exactly what keeps you stuck, you can then face your fear and take a step anyway. And that alone is an empowering decision in your life. We will take a close look at fear in chapter nine.

This is where trust in Spirit and the Universe comes in. This is when it's time to trust your Authentic Self, your Soul, the higher part of you that came here with all the answers. This is where your ego has the chance to be in a state of neutrality that says, "I am going to be okay no matter what the outcome. Things will go well for me, or I'll learn something." This is also where the newly formed belief system that says "Whatever happens is happening for the highest good of all concerned" is incredibly useful.

What if There Are No Wrong Decisions?

For every choice you make, there are always three potential outcomes:

Outcome #1: It will show you what you don't prefer so that you can become clearer on what you do prefer. Sometimes the best way to become clear on what you *do* want is to be shown what you *don't* want. When you can relax into this and add in the knowing that everything is happening for your learning, growth, and expansion, you can look at how things are unfolding and ask the question, "What is here for me?"

Outcome #2: The Universe will redirect you. The Universe is always directing us. It's simply a matter of if you choose to see it that way or if you fight it, holding on to what you want with a clenched fist and hanging on by your fingernails. This was certainly the old way of being for me. It was *my* way or the highway, as they say. I was absolutely being redirected by the Universe when I began coaching Nicola. Had I not followed through with the commitment I made to her, who knows what would have happened? The point is, the path unfolded before me based on the action I was taking, even though it seemed insignificant at the time.

Outcome #3: It will lead to the expansion you are seeking. Ahh, it's so great when things work out and go your way. See, here's the built-in promise of this: The more you believe that everything is happening *for* you, the more you will experience that things will *always* work out in your favor. ("Your favor" doesn't always mean that you get what you want.) After all, your beliefs create your world! I find that if I am clear in my intentions, without holding on to a particular outcome, it all flows. The right people show up, the road rises up to meet me, and a door always opens. Sometimes it's just not the door that I thought was going to open. Often, looking back, it seems like magic.

Can you see how all of this is just perspective?

In my own life, I remained stuck in a job I did not love for four years. While I knew that it was not where I wanted to be, it was *familiar*. Even though, at times, I was miserable and uncomfortable, the familiarity is what kept me there. In a twisted way, it was safe because I knew and understood the terrain. I (really, my ego) was unable to see all the steps or develop the plan to get me out of where I was. I was afraid to make the "wrong" move; therefore, I made no move at all. This "stuckness" then manifested itself in my life as a frozen shoulder and great emotional contraction. My lack of internal decision-making physically appeared as my frozen shoulder.

Once you make a decision and take action, the Universe can then make its move by either meeting you or redirecting you. When you begin to acknowledge the infinite part of your Being, the part of you that is all-knowing and that is connected to Source and All That Is, you begin to understand that from the Soul's perspective, there is *no such thing* as a wrong decision.

Spiritual Psychology underpins the idea that everything happening in our lives is perfectly designed for our learning, growth, expansion, and experience. Drs. Ron and Mary Hulnick teach, "Everything is FOR you." Therefore, I believe it doesn't really matter which path you take; it's just a matter of making a choice. "The system is rigged in your favor!" You cannot make a wrong move! Or, said in another way, the only wrong move is deciding *not* to move.

Hang Up the How

One of the hardest parts of decision-making is getting hung up on the *how*. This, again, is a planning strategy employed by your ego. It wants to check the database so it can see all the steps. You prevent yourself from deciding because you've forgotten how to dream. You don't allow yourself to imagine what would be amazing or what you would love, because your ego will get you stuck on *how* it's going to come about. This is a tricky tactic to keep you in your safe little comfort zone. You don't know what is *out there*, so you subconsciously talk yourself into staying *right here*. Here, in the place of *stuckness*.

So how do you get unstuck? Well, are you willing to consider that the *how* is not up to you? The how is actually not your job! Your only job is to be really, really clear on *what* you want and *why* you want it. Leave the *how* up to the Universe. Can you trust that you will be shown?

Remember, your logical/physical mind is only capable of observing how something has occurred or unfolded in the past. It is not designed to know how something will happen in the future. Only your Higher Self, or Spirit, knows "how" something will happen.

When I left my lucrative corporate career, I knew I wanted to do work in the world that made a difference on a broader scale. I knew *why* I wanted to do that: because it would give me more meaning, more purpose, and a sense of fulfillment. That is all I really knew. I did not know *how* to do this. The details got filled in for me by my Higher Self. My Authentic Self was leading the way and designing something that was far more than what I was capable of imagining on my own.

What do you really want to experience, and *why* do you want to experience something? What is your motivation for wanting it? Do you want more freedom and creativity and expression? Do you want to make a difference and to feel like you are living with purpose? Once I decided this for myself, the Universe knew it and went to work on my behalf. Even though I had no idea *how* to get there, the Universe did. It was my job to simply be clear about *what* I wanted to experience and *why* I wanted it.

When you can begin to see that everything is unfolding on behalf of your learning and growth, even when it might not look the way you thought it would, you can begin to enjoy the full experience of life.

One of the biggest lessons I learned at USM was that "Life is *for* you." Everything that is unfolding is part of what we came here to learn.

Are you willing to give yourself permission to take the self-imposed limitations *away*? Just allow yourself to imagine. Allow yourself to *dream*. What would you really love? What would be happening if you were living the most delicious, magical, fun, loving, life-expanding experience? What would provide you with all the joy and fulfillment you desire? How would you feel if you were living on purpose, making a difference, and feeling a sense of fulfillment?

Forget about the *how*. Focus on the *what*. Get clear on the *what*, and you begin summoning energy particles into waves and then into physical matter! The Universe does not like the hokey-pokey! It doesn't do "one foot in and one foot out." Create an energetic blueprint in your mind of what you want to experience and then commit your Life-Force energy to that. This is an inside job, an inward commitment to yourself. When you decide *what* you really want and *why* you want it, the Universe immediately conspires for you. Then your role is to make little choices and take tiny actions that move you in that direction.

The travelers of Israel used to cross the desert at night because it was cooler. They would pack up all of their belongings, animals, and kids, and they would cross in complete darkness. The only light they had were foot lamps that they tied to their ankles so that each step forward was illuminated. They could only *see* one step at a time.

This is what happened with me. I took one little step, and the next step was illuminated. It would have been nice to have had the whole path lit up for me, and I've found that that's not how it usually works. I continued to "feel" the steps I was taking. I developed trust.

Action is required! Unfortunately, you can't dream up a really beautiful picture of what you want to experience and then just sit on the couch. You live in this dense, physical, third-dimensional reality, and while ease and grace is possible, you still need to take the actual steps to move your life forward. You can receive *a lot* of assistance from your Higher Self and the Universe, and you have to make the first move. Mary Morrissey says, "Take one little step with what you have from where you are." What can you do today? What would you do today if you *believed* you could create your dream? How would your decisions be different?

The Inner and the Outer

Most of us are brought up to believe that the attainment of "things" is what life is about. Things, meaning both materials and achievements. Things you try to attain both outside of you and inside of you. Consider that everything you need is actually already in you. We all set out to our individual destinations in order to acquire objects and people and things and stuff. Then maybe we get what we were looking for, or maybe we don't.

And the truth is that what we are really looking for is *underneath* all of those things. We are really looking for the feelings that those things will bring us. This is why you can look at *what* you want and, more importantly, *why* you want something. Do you believe that a nice house will boost your self-worth? Will finding the right partner bring you security and completeness? Maybe, but only for a minute. The older you get, the more you will realize the attainment of things in the outer world cannot provide the *lasting fulfillment* you are really searching for.

What I have learned in my fifty-two years so far is that what you want is not the *outer* experience, which takes place in physical reality; instead, what you really want is the *inner* experience, which takes place inside of you. This is what you are truly seeking. You buy into the misunderstanding that only the attainment of things will bring you the joy, peace, happiness, security, meaning, purpose, and fulfillment you desire. The more you attain the outer "things," however, the more you realize they don't usually align with your inner desires.

In the never-ending search for things, you become a rat on a wheel. I certainly did. How do you stop the madness? You return to the beginning. You stop the *doing* and check in with your *Being*. You remember that you are a creator—an incredible, multidimensional Being—and that acknowledging yourself that way can invoke reverence and awe of your true essence. Return inward, recognize your authentic nature as the energy of Love, and honor the decision you made to embark on an epic human adventure as a spiritual Being. It is the expression of your unique, individualized energy that is your purpose, which is part of the greater whole.

Opportunity for Transformation
Take Action

This is the third Opportunity for Transformation. This is your chance to take action and move your life forward, discover a new part of your consciousness, and create an experience for yourself that will deepen your learning of this material. All of the OFTs are designed to assist you in more fully integrating Original Wisdom from your Authentic Self into your day-to-day life. If you would like to download an actual worksheet or listen to an audio version of this OFT, please visit donnabond.com/opportunityfortransformation.

What Do You Want, and Why Do You Want It?

Consider that the *how* is not up to you. Consider that the Universe owns that part. Your job is to get really clear on the *what* and the *why*. What do you want, and why do you want it? This process is only complete when you consider this question both *outside* of you and, most importantly, *inside* of you. In other words, what do you want to see happening in your outer world, your physical reality? This is your health, relationships, career, finance, and home life. This is your outer world in the physical.

When things occur in your outer world, you have experiences that can only take place inside of you. This is your *inner* world. This is how you think and feel about what is happening in the outer world. For example, you think that a certain career brings you a sense of achievement and success or that certain relationships make you feel peaceful, loved, meaningful, etc. Perhaps your finances inspire a feeling of safety or abundance. Maybe your home life inspires a sense of harmony and flow.

When you pursue something in the physical world, it's mostly because you are really looking for what you will experience inside yourself.

The Process:

Getting Crystal Clear on the "What"

Find a pen you love and a good notebook or a special journal. Set aside some quality time for this work. Before you begin, get quiet. Listen to your breath. Connect to your Life Force. Ask your Authentic Self for assistance and answer the following questions:

When you consider the experience you'd like to have in this life, how would you like to feel on the inside?

Abundant	Empowered	Loved
Accepting Life	Enthusiastic	Meaningful
As It Is	Excellent	Mindful
Accessing	Friendship	Neutral
Original Wisdom	Fulfilled	On Purpose
Achievement	Generous	Oneness
Aligned	Grateful	Patient
Alive	Grounded	Peaceful
Appreciative	Guided	Present
Authentic	Happy	Protected
Being in the Flow	Harmonious	Safe
Being of Service	Heart-Centered	Secure
Calm	Humorous	Self-Aware
Cherished	Important	Self-Love
Compassionate	Inner-Esteem	Self-Mastery

Confident	Joyful	Self-Reliance
Connected	Kind	Self-Worth
Soulful	Trustworthy	Uplifted
Supported	Understood	Valuing Self
Surrendered	Uninhibited	
Synchronistic	Self-Expression	
Trust of Self	Unique	

WHAT does the outer experience look like?

In each of the major categories below, consider what you would love to occur in your *outer* experience. Begin each sentence with "I AM." (For example, I AM in a relationship with the man of my dreams, I AM financially abundant, I AM healthy and energetic, and so on.)

Spirituality and Personal Growth

Romance and Partnership

Leisure and Recreation

Money and Finances

Family and Friends

Home and Environment

Health and Well-Being

Career

WHY do you want the experience?

Consider that you seek to attain something for the feeling it will bring you. (For example: To know and feel that you are making a difference in the world. To experience the joy, upliftment, and support from a loving and balanced relationship.) Certainly, this is not an exhaustive list. Perhaps tune into your own guidance before exploring these prompts.

Acceptance	Encouragement	Needed
Admiration	Enthusiasm	Nostalgic
Affection	Euphoric	Optimistic
Appreciative	Exalted	Passionate
Aliveness	Excited	Pleased
Altruism	Exhilarated	Pleasurable
Amazement	Fantastic	Qualified
Amusement	Fine	Reborn
Appreciated	Fit	Rejuvenated
At Ease	Friendly	Relaxed
Awe	Flow	Relieved
Blissful	Glad	Reverence
Balance	Glorious	Satisfied
Calm	Gracious	Serenity
Capable	Grand	Strength
Certain	Grateful	Successful
Cheerfulness	Gratified	Supported
Cherished	Happy	Sure
Clarity	Hopeful	Tender
Comfortable	Honored	Thrilled
Compassion	Impactful	Trusting
Confidence	Important	Trustworthy
Contribution	Inspired	Unique
Creativity	Irresistible	Uplifted
Curiosity	Joyful	Warmhearted
Delight	Kindness	Well-Being
Difference	Loveable	Worthwhile
Eagerness	Loved	
Elevation	Loving	
Empowerment	Meaningful	

Now, tune into your Authentic Self for guidance and answer these inner inquiries:

What would you love to do and share, and why?

What places do you want to see and explore, and why?

What does the house of your dreams look like, and why?

What is the exact amount of debt you want to pay off, and why?

What do you love to contribute your time to, and why?

What dreams do you have for your kids, and why?

What dream did you have as a kid that's still in there, and why?

What choices matter to you, and why?

What is your vision for the milestones in your life, and why?

Which person would you most love to hang out with on the planet, and why?

What kind of wealth do you want to create, and why?

What kind of legacy do you want to leave behind, and why?

What makes your heart sing, and why?

What brings you feelings of enthusiasm, and why?

What would you do for free, and why?

Sacred Truth Activation

This is the third Sacred Truth Activation. Find a quiet, private space to center yourself, light a candle, and speak these words aloud. If you would like to listen to an audio version of this guided personal decree, please visit donnabond.com/sacredtruthactivations.

I Am Moving My Life Forward by Making Decisions

I am aware that I chose to take on a bodily form and come into this life. As I take ownership for this choice, I move away from victimhood and move onto the path of victory. I am aware that my life moves forward because of the choices and decisions I make. I am aware that if I choose not to make a decision, I have still made a choice. I am aware that my life is filled with many choices each and every day, and as I take responsibility for the choices I make, I empower myself. I am empowered to make decisions from a place of love and peace and expansion. I am choosing to feel authentically empowered by making choices to move my life forward.

I am mindfully attuned to the decisions I make. I use my intuitive guidance to see, hear, sense, and feel my options as a way to guide my life. I slow down. I become fully present, and I connect to the choices I have in front of me. I align myself with this choice inwardly and notice how I feel when I make this decision. I am aware that choices that are in alignment with my highest and best good make me feel lighter and more expansive. Inside of me, these choices give me feelings of upliftment and freedom. I am also aware that when I tune in and imagine making a choice that invokes a feeling of contraction or restriction, I interpret that direction as being out of alignment with my inner knowing.

I am confident in the decisions I make, knowing that all the decisions are perfect for where I am now. I am making decisions that move my life forward in a way that is divinely designed for me. I fully and completely trust that all of the decisions I make lead to growth that is perfect for my life's evolution. I am aware that there are no "wrong" decisions. I am aware that I am always safe on the learning path of my life. I am an infinite, divine, energetic Being, and I am trusting myself to make decisions that represent what I've learned in this life.

The search for the Holy Grail was the literal search for the chalice that Jesus Christ supposedly used at the Last Supper. People believed this lost treasure would cure all ills and bestow great wealth. For eons of time, we humans have been in search of the sacred Holy Grail, believing it is something outside *of us that will offer the completeness we seek—a sense of purpose, wholeness, and fulfillment. Perhaps the real Holy Grail is the pure essence of Love* inside *each one of us. It is not something to be discovered at a destination, but rather, it's a wellspring in the blossom of the unfolding.*

The entelechy of an apple seed is an apple tree—or for this initiate, an entire apple orchard! Entelechy is the natural unfolding that occurs from the inside out, transforming into the fullest realized expression of something. The entelechy of an acorn is an oak tree. The entelechy of a caterpillar is a butterfly.

Until awakened, the initiate lives her life asleep, unaware of the Original Wisdom that her personal Holy Grail exists within the natural unfolding of herself and her life. In truth, she is in search of herself and the fullest realized expression of her unique, individualized energy. The energy she is made from, called Love.

Chapter Four

Expression Is Your Purpose

"Entelechy is all about the possibilities
encoded in each one of us."

~ Jean Houston

When I entered the two-year master's program, I initially never considered completing the third year, which was an adjunct to the Spiritual Psychology degree. It was called Consciousness, Health, and Healing. It never occurred to me to do it, even as I neared graduation. I had just invested $30,000 and a lot of time into two years of school. I had walked away from my high-paying career and was now beginning my journey as an entrepreneur and marketing consultant, learning how to generate income without the safety net of a bi-weekly paycheck.

Months earlier, I was reading Jean Houston's book *The Wizard of Us*, which was a gift from my dear friend Mary Grace, and I came across the word *entelechy*. I didn't know what it meant, so I got up out of bed to look it up on yourdictionary.com.

En·tel·e·chy: The complete realization and final form of some potential concept or function; the conditions under which a potential thing becomes actualized.

I returned to reading my book, and there was something about this new word that felt electric to me. It was alive inside of me, yet I didn't really understand why. The very next day, I received an email from USM, and in it Dr. Mary Hulnick was talking about how each of us has an entelechy. I learned that the entelechy of an acorn, for example, is an oak tree. Hidden almost like a code within each one of us is this yet-to-be-realized potential that is waiting to be ignited.

For the third day in a row, the word entelechy appeared before me, this time in my horoscope. I thought this was an incredible synchronicity, so I saved Mary's e-mail and my horoscope, thinking no one would believe this occurrence. As always, I clearly acknowledged the magic that was unfolding, but at the time I didn't know why it was happening.

It was one of the last weekends in the two-year program, and Drs. Ron and Mary Hulnick had set aside time to talk about the curriculum for the Consciousness, Health, and Healing program. Again, I had *no intention* of attending this program. I had done enough. I was complete. I listened with a neutral ear, unaffected by what they said about the program that was affectionately referred to as CHH. That is, until Mary began talking about her favorite class within her favorite program. She practically sang the word as her smooth, velvet voice harmonically permeated my Being. "My favorite class in this curriculum is called Entelechy."

What did she just say? Time wrinkled just a bit, and I thought to myself, *Did I hear her correctly?* The description of the class went into the ether because I didn't hear another word after that. Entelechy. In that moment, I recognized I was being guided. There are no accidents, and I don't believe in coincidences. This was clear, undeniable direction from my Higher Self, and it was inviting me into Consciousness, Health, and Healing. While I didn't know it at the time, I was being invited into the unfolding of my own entelechy. I have learned in this journey that oftentimes I need to be hit in the head with a poster-board-sized announcement in order to understand my next step.

Times like this, when the Universe communicated with me, were super helpful when I was learning how to break out of my left-brained, analytical, logical mind.

I enrolled in the third year. The most difficult part about this was explaining to my husband that I was going *back in* for year three! After months of building up fear in my own mind that he would be mad, he lovingly supported me. He somehow knew year three was going to be my biggest breakthrough. And it was. Today, I hold a master's degree in Spiritual Psychology with an emphasis in Consciousness, Health, and Healing.

Awakening to Your Life Purpose

When I turned forty-four, which is how old my father was when he died, it became glaringly obvious that nothing was more important in my life than making the journey of self-discovery and inner exploration. I didn't realize then that the seed that had always remained dormant within me was awakening and that it was time to cultivate it. What took me all that time to figure out was that *my purpose* was the process of cultivating that seed from germination to emergence.

Our lives' events reveal specific timing and conditions that activate our Souls' growth and purpose at different stages throughout our lives. For me, that particular moment was when I was ready to really take responsibility for what gives me life, what makes me come alive, and what brings me joy.

Answering the inner question "What is true for *me*?" became a main part of the discovery process itself. What was true for me was not necessarily what my parents taught me, or my schools, or church, or society. I needed to discover what was real for me, independent of all of those influences. I had pursued the corporate ladder; I had pursued and obtained the money and power and prestige. I had the recognition and the bonus checks and the vacations, and guess what? THAT WASN'T IT! OMG! Discovering this was like realizing my whole life had been a farce! And I am getting ahead of myself.

The reason most people don't go out and just "create" what they would love in their lives is because most of us don't really know what that is. And mostly, we don't do it, because we don't believe we can. So, here is a little wake-up call: THIS IS YOUR LIFE, AND IT'S PRETTY SHORT! You are far more creative, resourceful, resilient, amazing, and powerful than you've given yourself credit for. Stop buying into all the crap you've been told by other people! How do you choose to devote your time? What are you called to infuse your drop-of-God energy with? How do you choose to live your life? Isn't *your* fleeting, precious, gone-in-a-nanosecond *life* a good enough reason to recognize your inherent Original Wisdom, figure out what you love, and figure out how to experience more of that?

The purpose of your life is to be *you*. The true you is the highest frequency of the energy of Love that you express. Your purpose is the uncovering and discovering, the birthing and blossoming, and the expression and experience of the *true you* in your unique human form. Your purpose is to live and *be* the Authentic You. The purpose of your life is to bring forth the Love that you are, regardless of the many people, situations, and circumstances that have influenced you. It takes great courage to make this discovery within yourself and to live as the fullest realized version of yourself. Every single one of us shares this purpose.

Your Authentic Self is the part of you that intuitively *knows* how life wants to express itself through you so that your expression is laced with joy, happiness, and fulfillment. The Love that you are essentially gets covered up and buried by all the layers of patterning and beliefs that get piled upon you when you incarnate as a physical Being and live a human life in the physical reality. You are born knowing the truth of your Authentic Self; this is your Original Wisdom. As you grow up, you forget this truth. The purpose of your life is to return to this universal truth—to remember it, really—the truth that you are a multidimensional, spiritual Being on a human adventure. You can do this through a process of discovery and excavation. You examine each of the beliefs that are operating your life and study them to determine if they are really true in your heart or if, perhaps, these beliefs are something you have adopted along the way because of your parents, and their parents, and their parents, and theirs.

Clues of Misalignment

When you are off track in the fulfillment of your highest purpose—your entelechy—your life can feel out of balance. A key indicator is when your head and your heart are out of alignment. This key indicator portends a much greater opportunity for joy and fulfillment in your life. When you become aware of misalignment in your life, you can meet these imbalances as your Soul's learning journey. You can reframe obstacles as learning opportunities. When you're misaligned, the following experiences may be prevalent:

1. **You *mentally* feel out of alignment with the life you are living.** You may have pursued (and achieved) goals and then realized they were someone else's. You did what you thought you "should" do. You find yourself thinking about being somewhere else or doing something else and find your attention fragmented. It's hard to focus, and in your own mind you lack clarity. You realize that you may have been living your life according to someone else's rules or belief system. Just because you were born into a certain family, religion, culture, or heritage, it does not mean that all of the cultural beliefs that exist within that "tribe" are going to resonate deep in your heart as *your* truth.

2. **You *physically* feel unwell.** You may have a low energy level, or you may even be suffering from a physical imbalance. You may be suffering from an illness or a disease. You may have a low-tolerant immune system and easily catch every sniffle you walk by. You may get into frequent "accidents." You may be powering your physical body with pharmaceuticals, taking pills to go to sleep, to wake up, or simply to get through the day.

3. **You *emotionally* feel unhappy, unsatisfied, and unfulfilled.** When you tune in to your heart, you feel a strong sense of discontent. Even when things may look great on the surface (a high-paying job, a nice car, a spouse, and a couple of kids), you may feel sad or depressed and feel consumed by negative thoughts. Your relationships with others may be strained or broken. You may be numbing yourself with drugs or alcohol.

4. **You *spiritually* feel disconnected from yourself and from a Higher Power.** You may be missing a connection to nature and other people. Your life may lack flow and a sense of purpose, fulfillment, and direction.

All of us are brought up with many external influences in life. These influences played a large role in shaping your belief system, and some still do today. It's easy to see how you have been "taught" who to be, what to believe, how to be, and what to do. As you review this list and consider what I am sharing, I want to be a voice for the idea that everyone (and everything) on this list is really just doing the best they can. And all of these influences are providing a perfect learning opportunity for your Soul. Some of these influences include:

- Parents
- Media
- Society
- Teachers
- Culture
- Nation

- Tribe
- Race
- Ethnicity
- Religion
- Nationality

Because of the learned beliefs you adopt from all of these external forces and more, you unknowingly cover up or bury your Authentic Self. In other words, the spiritual Being that you are—in all its magnificence and glory—gets camouflaged by all of the patterning that occurs through the many influences in your life that are telling you who and how to be. (Like many of my clients, for example, who were deeply entrenched in religious beliefs that disempowered their true expression.) These internal traps are sometimes created, causing you to buy into misunderstandings, such as the idea that it's wrong to get divorced or to be gay. When you have buried your Authentic Self and you are ignoring the whispers of your Original Wisdom, the outside world around you will mirror the confusion and misalignment you are carrying around on the inside. Getting the mental, physical, emotional, and spiritual aspects of yourself in alignment is a *vital* component of living your truth and enjoying a fulfilling life. Misalignment can look like:

- Physical problems
- Mental problems/depression
- Relationship problems
- Financial problems
- Emotional problems

Decoding Your Assignments

As many spiritual teachers have taught for eons of time, life itself is the Soul's classroom. Gary Zukuv—an American spiritual teacher and the author of four consecutive *New York Times* bestsellers, including *The Seat of the Soul*—refers to life as "Earth school." Drs. Ron and Mary Hulnick say, "All of life is for learning." I've heard Robert Ohotto—the author of the bestselling book *Transforming Fate into Destiny*, a world-renowned radio show host, and an intuitive consultant—comment, "All has value." We are all here for our growth and learning as well as for the continued evolution of our Souls' growth and the evolution of humanity. While I've read about this from many spiritual teachers, and while I learned more about it in my master's program, it was my Original Wisdom that recognized this as truth. It was as if these spiritual teachers were reflecting what is true inside of me, and my only job was to recognize that.

Together, we continue to awaken in the awareness of our spiritual heritage as a humanity. We are all here "on assignment." All who have taken embodiment are blossoming into the fullest expression of their selves toward their entelechy. We are each given repeated opportunities to learn the lessons we came into this world to learn. For example, one of my biggest learnings is that the longer I am on the spiritual path, the more I am aware that it's about loving my humanness.

So, how do you figure out your individual "lesson plans?" (And it is plural. It seems like we all came here to learn many things.) I have found that learning how "projection" works has really assisted me and my clients in "seeing" and understanding the learning opportunities that are literally right in front of us. Projection is a term used in psychology. I learned about projection at USM. Healthline.com explains projection in this way: Projection refers to unconsciously taking unwanted emotions or traits you don't like about yourself and attributing them to someone else.

Goodtherapy.org gives this useful explanation and example: Projection is a psychological defense mechanism in which individuals attribute characteristics they find unacceptable in themselves to another person. For example, a husband who has a hostile nature might see and experience his wife as hostile or perceive her as angry.

Life is a mirror. The opportunities you can use to transform yourself and to learn the lessons you came here to learn are essentially right in front of you. And you often don't "see" your life lessons, because you think (you project) the problem onto others. Drs. Ron and Mary Hulnick teach, "Outer experience is a reflection of inner reality," and what that means is that what is happening inside of yourself, in your consciousness and subconscious, is mirrored back to you through the events, situations, and circumstances in your life.

When I had the opportunity to work directly with my own projections at the University of Santa Monica, it was enlightening to understand how I was so out of balance. I started to "see" my own life lessons. How? One way was by slowing down and looking at what I was saying about others. "He should stop doing that!" *Oh, I'm the one who needs to stop doing that.* "She needs to start taking care of herself!" *Oh, I need to start taking care of myself.*

You can *see* when others are dishonoring the whispers of their hearts and when they are being unfaithful to what is true in the core of their Beings. It is even harder to *see* it in yourself. If you are willing to slow down and learn about how projection works, you can experience the "shock" and "joy" that comes from realizing that your "upsets" with and about other people actually point you to learning opportunities in *your* own life. When you are out of balance, you may find your "buttons being pushed" in a particular area. This is a clear sign that the opportunity for growth is being presented. Identifying the distinction between a healing opportunity and your "buttons getting pushed" is not an easy concept for your ego. Actually, your ego (your learned self) doesn't like it at all, because it likes to be right. Owning your projections invites you to take 100 percent of the responsibility for the experiences you are having in your life. Owning your projections means that when you get upset about someone, you are willing to consider that *you* may be behaving the exact same way in the relationship you have with *yourself* or in the relationships you have with others.

The ego would much prefer for you *not* to look at your own "faults and weaknesses." The ego would prefer for you to continue the "blame game" and scapegoat tactics. That is why seeing life as a mirror is one of the more challenging growth concepts to work with. One of the best ways to understand projections is to look at it in the positive. Your ego can "try this on" in an easier way. When you see someone you really admire or are inspired by, you naturally feel uplifted and enthusiastic. You may even feel touched emotionally and have feelings of love and admiration toward the person. You find it easy to quickly recognize all of the amazing qualities and attributes that this person is reflecting to you. Well, think about it like this: You hold within *you* the same qualities and attributes that you see in the other person. If you didn't have those qualities, you wouldn't be able to recognize them. You may have trouble "owning" these positive qualities inside yourself, which is why it's easier for you to *project* them on someone else.

When someone "pushes your buttons" and you get upset because of his or her actions, it's likely that you are somehow demonstrating (or thinking about) this same type of behavior. The key here is that this is an opportunity to become aware of how you are thinking, feeling, and/or acting when someone else "gets you upset." When you feel set off emotionally, the other person is simply the mirror in your movie. The "inner turmoil" is the key to uncovering how you are relating to yourself. If you're emotionally charged by those who refuse to cooperate, it may be because of your own reluctance to cooperate with others, or perhaps you're not cooperating with some aspect of yourself. If you are fired up by people who betray you, ask yourself if you have a tendency to abandon others or yourself. If you are judgmental about how hard the boss is driving the team, turn the mirror toward yourself, inquire within, and see how hard you are on others or maybe yourself.

Let's look deeper at a popular example: criticism from a parent. When your parents criticize, you tend to have a strong negative response to them. My mother may be trying to help, though in a clumsy way, when she lets me know that she likes my hair better when it is longer or when she tells me it looks like I've put on a few pounds. Ouch! When I step away from this and think about it, I may conclude something like this: My mother doesn't approve of the way I look. However, if I turn this around and look at how this is my own projection, I may realize that "I don't approve of myself."

This then invites you to look at your judgments and positionality. *The judgments you have of others are really judgments you have of yourself.* They can also be connected to something deeper, such as the belief that "I'm not good enough." The judgment that you are placing on yourself is hurtful and unsupportive, and it's a way that you communicate lack of acceptance of who you are. What would it be like if you were on your own team?

The introduction in *A Course in Miracles,* the sacred text scribed by Helen Schucman, states, "The course does not aim at teaching the meaning of love, for that is beyond what can be taught. It does aim, however, at removing the blocks to the awareness of love's presence, which is your natural inheritance. The opposite of love is fear, but what is all-encompassing can have no opposite." Drs. Ron and Mary Hulnick teach that all of our judgments are blocks to the Love that we are.

To move toward having self-compassion and gentleness for your sweet self is a courageous and heart-centered way of being. The subtleties and metaphoric references reflecting what we are here to learn about life are everywhere. Everything in life has value. It's all for your continued expansion, and you are constantly being given feedback by your surroundings.

When you can step away from what I call "being in the blender," you have the opportunity to gain perspective. When you are "in the blender," you are caught up in the drama of the emotion. You are "in it," and there is no perspective. This promotes a tendency to react. When you step back, you can see the swirling unfolding in your life, and you have the space you need in order to choose your response. It is a sure sign that "earth school is in session," and a growth opportunity is being presented when someone else "gets you upset." When you can take the seat of the observer, step back from the blender, and watch the upset instead of being "in it," you can use the tools of Spiritual Psychology to generate a meaningful inner inquiry.

I have a client who recently found herself falling down and hurting herself repeatedly. I asked her to reflect on this inquiry: "How am I constantly beating myself up?" She gained the awareness that she was staying in a relationship that was emotionally abusive. Once she realized the connection and moved into having self-compassion about her decision, she was able to see the situation more clearly and make a different choice.

From the Soul's perspective, everyone is on their own learning journey. You are given perfectly designed experiences that present you with opportunities to learn the lessons you came into this world to learn. The Soul does not make judgments about what is right or wrong, good or bad. Only your ego does that, as it is trapped in a world of duality. Your Soul is here, living on Planet Earth, for the *experience*. We forget that we are divine, spiritual Beings having a human adventure.

Gary Zukuv says, "The Earth school is not a concept. It is an ongoing 3-dimesional, full color, hi-fidelity, interactive multimedia experience that does not end until your Soul goes home (until you die). Every moment in the Earth school offers you important opportunities to learn about yourself. Those things have to do with your Soul. The Earth school operates with exquisite perfection and efficiency whether you are aware of it or not."

The higher you raise your consciousness, the more you naturally reside in the Love that you are. Your Soul's essence is pure, Divine Love. The unresolved issues you carry with you are what block you from recognizing the Love that you are. Your judgments are the keys to unlocking and dissolving the issues within you. If you are not triggered by something, that is an indication that "it just is," and it is not a healing opportunity within your own consciousness. The more you can free yourself from your emotional turmoil and move away from judgment and toward acceptance, the more enjoyable and fulfilling the adventure will be.

When you are walking around in the world experiencing negative emotions, the natural by-product is that you feel bad. This occurs on all levels: mental, emotional, physical, and spiritual. When you are in your natural essence, vibrating as the energy of Love, you feel great. When someone "pushes your buttons," it's the perfect opportunity for self-reflection and a perception shift. Your life is a reflection of what's going on inside of you. The quality of your relationships with others is a direct mirror of the relationship you have with yourself. By recognizing these instances in which you are aware of an imbalance—as well as when you find your buttons being pushed—you can decode your assignments or learning opportunities on the spot. This is very empowering.

Your Soul Has the Map

Even if your outer world is imbalanced, and even if you can't isolate what is wrong, inside of you, there is a calm, gentle, and intelligent sense of peace in the form of your guidance system, and it is trying to get your attention. The upside is that somewhere, somehow, you begin to feel the pull (or perhaps "hear the call") toward a more joyful, fulfilling life that feels *purposeful*. Deep within your Being, you believe that there is something else—something more, something bigger—that you are connected to and are part of. Your Soul, as Gary Zukuv points

out—this positive, purposeful force at the core of your Being—
is giving you clues and messages about your specific discovery
process, which includes the lessons you are here to learn as well
as the clues you need in order to cultivate the seed of your entelechy. As evidence, your Soul—your Authentic Self—infuses
energy into areas of your life and into your personality that are
inviting your attention.

The first step in this unfolding is to move toward feeling
good. As you approach life's experiences, you are always taking
in information. You can pay attention to whether an experience
makes you expand or contract. Does the experience make you
grow or shrivel? Does it make you feel nourished or depleted?
As you experience your life, paying attention to these signs is key
in helping you distinguish the truth of your higher Being. The
secret to your own personal discovery and authentic delivery
of who you really are (and your happiness and fulfillment) is to
align your thoughts, emotions, and actions with the highest
part of yourself, your Infinite Intelligence, your Soul, your
Original Wisdom.

Consider that your life, and everything that happens within
it, is the *Soul's curriculum*. In other words, your Soul signed up
for *everything* that is happening in your life, for the sole purpose of experiencing the opportunities and learning the lessons
in your assignment. Through the lens of the Soul, you are here
to experience and to learn. The Soul is here for all aspects of
an experience and holds no positionality, attachment, expectations, or judgment about the experience you are having. When
you look through the lens of the Soul, you see only Love. This
is hard for your ego and personality to come to terms with. If,
in this lifetime, your Soul chooses to learn about forgiveness,

you will enter life situations in which you may be betrayed. If your Soul chooses to learn about humility, it's likely you will experience humiliation. Clearing the filter of judgment allows Love to shine through everything you see, inviting you to view things differently. It is only in your humanness that you judge betrayal as bad or wrong or something you wouldn't "sign up for." Yet the Soul asks, "What is here for me?" Everything that is happening in your life is beautifully orchestrated to provide you with learning opportunities so that your Soul can evolve.

Your Soul has the map. I imagine my Soul Map is always out ahead of me. Our Souls are always getting us where we need to go, presenting us with what we need to experience in order to learn the lessons we came here to learn. Our Souls are also communicating with us through what we are interested in, through the clues of misalignment, and through the things that make us feel uplifted.

Birthing You Is Why You're Here

Your life can be likened to an assignment that is a grand experiment being carried out by your Soul. Before your Soul entered a body, you designed the opportunities that would give you the best chance to fulfill the spiritual curriculum you intended to learn in this life. I have learned through my own personal journey that nothing is more important than the discovery and the delivery of who you really are, coming into alignment with that authentic Being, and then living your life from that place. Exploration, revelation, and declaration of the true *you*, the Authentic You, and expressing that which makes you come alive is what life is all about. As a spiritual Being having a human adventure, THIS IS YOUR PRIMARY JOB!

You came here to discover your true essence, which is pure Love. You came here to experience your spiritual nature while you're in your human form. You came here with an agenda to learn life lessons (your assignments). You came to see everything and everyone through the lens of Love. And perhaps you came to learn lessons about understanding, humility, and forgiveness, to name a few. The only way your Soul can experience these lessons is by taking a physical form on Earth and experiencing the physical world and all its polarities through each of your five senses.

You are here to experience the ups and downs of the rollercoaster ride that makes up your life. And make no mistake, you did not come here simply for a ride; you came here on *assignment*. Each of our assignments are unique, and we also share assignments with the collective human consciousness. For example, we are *all* here to learn about love. However, each one of us is here to experience the fullness of our entelechy. Your individual Soul Purpose is unique and is what is true inside of you, and it wants to be expressed out in the world.

Discovering who you really are, along with the birthing of your Authentic Self, is done by connecting to the things you really love and that bring you joy. The exploration, revelation, and declaration of the things that make you come alive is why you are here. This is what is means to "follow your bliss." This is part of *everyone's* assignment. Through this journey, this awakening, you have the realization (or shall we say, the remembering) that you really are a divine Being that is connected to Spirit, and you are made up of and connected to Source energy; you are that Source energy, and that energy vibrates at the frequency of love. Self-expression is where happiness resides. This is not a destination; it's a way of life.

It's time to come into alignment with this Higher Intelligence, this Life Force, and realize it is not only connected to you; it is also who you are. This Intelligence resides within you and is accessible to you all the time. You are the one who gave yourself your earthly assignments from the realm of your Higher Self, your Authentic Self, your Soul.

This idea that your Soul is the part of you participating in your lesson plan gives you permission to accept that your life is happening according to an overall greater plan or divine design, the details of which are mostly unknown to you. And this "forgetting" of your spiritual nature is on purpose. Imagine it like planning a vacation. You know where you want to go and some of what you want to do, and you allow yourself room for spontaneity and surprise. Would you really want to go on a vacation or an adventure knowing everything that was going to happen? Not knowing enables you to have experiences, learn the intended lessons, and have the greatest revelations. It leaves room for the joy of discovering your Authentic Self along the journey. And you get to experience firsthand the empowering transformation in consciousness when you move from a place of limitation to one of expansion and freedom. This cannot be done from the Spirit Realm, as the Soul itself is nothing but conscious, expansive energy. So, this Infinite Intelligence sends to Earth a traveler—you—on this experiential journey. And throughout your life, you receive guidance and clues for the big agenda items of your Soul's plan.

The idea that you come in with a life-lesson plan is not to be confused with free will, because in all situations and circumstances, *you always have the power of choice.* How you choose to navigate your human adventure is always your choice. The way I interpret this is that if you came to this life to learn about being generous, you may have a propensity for being stingy, and life will set up scenarios in which you have the opportunity to demonstrate generosity. The set-up of the potential scenarios may be prearranged in some way, and you always have the free will to decide how to respond to the learning opportunity, and you can choose which scenarios you experience through the choices you make.

Realizing Your Entelechy

Ever since I was sixteen, I have been fascinated with all things mystical, metaphysical, and spiritual. What are the things and the topics that really make you come alive? What ideas make you feel expansive? What do you *love* learning about? Do you feel enthusiastic when you make discoveries about yourself and your own growth process? What invokes *pure joy* inside you? My girlfriends reminded me that on the way to school I used to quiz everyone on what they dreamed of the night before, and I would then assist in interpreting their dreams. I have been a Spiritual junkie since I was a teen. It took a long time before it occurred to me that teaching and sharing these concepts was *it* for me. Spirituality is what makes me feel expansive. I light up and feel enthusiastic. Metaphysics and psychology are what I love. What modality out there have you devoured? Have you ever looked for the answers that would unlock the secrets of *you*? I promise you will not find it in any book! This discovery is an inside job.

In my house, while growing up, we were taught that only hard work and sacrifice could lead to prosperity and abundance. So, that is what my influencers taught me and what I grew up believing, as many of us do. Have you ever questioned the "rules" you received growing up? Did you follow the plan of going off to college, getting a degree, and spending the next two decades climbing a ladder, believing that that was the way you were *supposed* to live life? Have you ever felt like you were forcing yourself to find a "sensible" career with job opportunities, industry advancement, and upward mobility?

What I didn't realize as I climbed my way up, was that with each step I unconsciously covered up what I really loved: spirituality, metaphysics, and *my* true expression of these ideas. Because of that, I was slowly dying inside. It was only a matter of time before this imbalance showed up in my life, revealing itself as a series of mental, physical, emotional, and spiritual inequities in my life. My revelation and discovery came when I stopped hiding what really made me come alive.

In the corporate arena, there was no room for metaphysics (or so I thought at the time), so I locked "Spirit Girl" in the closet. I hid her for so long because I had a misbelief that it wasn't socially acceptable. That it was a taboo subject to talk about, let alone have a career in. Now that I am aware that it's my truth and inspiration, I care much less about what other people say and think. I have realized my own truth and what is in alignment for me.

It's your Authentic Self that beckons you to grow. It invites feelings of freedom. It invites you to share! You are here to follow your joy and to give your attention to the things that summon your aliveness. These things are to be cultivated to realize your entelechy. This is the Life Force's invitation to more fully express yourself. Have you ever sensed into a feeling of expansiveness and known it was a whisper from your Soul, from your Higher Self, inviting you to go in a particular direction? Can you give yourself permission to pursue things that lead to feelings of expansion that are part of the recipe of what brings you the joy and fulfillment you seek? Think of these feelings of joy and expansion as a line of energy. They have a frequency to them. Are you ready to feel better? Are you ready to feel alive? As an energetic Being, you can flow with or against your innate stream of energy. When in alignment, this energy naturally activates the seed that becomes the blossom. The blossom that becomes the fruit of your fullest expression. Your entelechy.

Opportunity for Transformation
Take Action

This is the fourth Opportunity for Transformation. This is your chance to take action and move your life forward, discover a new part of your consciousness, and create an experience for yourself that will deepen your learning of this material. All of the OFTs are designed to assist you in more fully integrating Original Wisdom from your Authentic Self into your day-to-day life. If you would like to download an actual worksheet or listen to an audio version of this OFT, please visit donnabond.com/opportunityfortransformation.

Identifying Life Lesson Themes

In your journal, based on your life thus far, what are some of the themes or life lessons you sense you are learning? What are the areas of discontent for you? Look at patterns that repeat throughout your life. This is a big clue. Do you have emotional upset in a particular area?

Examples of patterns could include:

- Transforming judgment into acceptance.
- Transforming intolerance into understanding.
- Transforming indifference into mastery.
- Transforming dishonor into graciousness.
- Transforming blame into forgiveness.
- Transforming victimization into freedom.
- Transforming doubt into curiosity.
- Transforming arrogance into humility
- Transforming half-heartedness into commitment and devotion.
- Transforming conflict into peace.
- Transforming self-sacrifice into self-love.

Patterns (and we all have more than one, of course) could include speaking your voice, sharing your truth, acknowledging yourself, or facing your fears. I may suggest that at the root of all of your patterns are opportunities to love and accept yourself. For example, many of my clients, myself included, are frequently trapped in judgment. (A casualty of being human, unfortunately.) We judge everything because we've somehow fallen into the trap of thinking, on some level, that things "should be" different than what they are. This can be applied to a person, a situation, or a circumstance. You name it. When you constantly judge everything and everyone around you, resistance is created, which in turn creates suffering because there is an insistence that things be other than what they really are. This presents the learning opportunity for acceptance.

Step 1: Identify your patterns.

Step 2: What do you sense are the life-learning opportunities that are being offered as a response to the patterns you are identifying?

Journal about any awareness that is present for you.

Sacred Truth Activation

This is the fourth Sacred Truth Activation. Find a quiet, private space to center yourself, light a candle, and speak these words aloud. If you would like to listen to an audio version of this guided personal decree, please visit donnabond.com/sacredtruthactivations.

I Am Birthing the True Expression of Me

I am on the planet to birth the true expression of me, the authentic me, the truth of me. I am aware that I chose to be here in this life, at this time, on this planet. I know that all of the situations and circumstances in my life are perfectly designed to assist me in discovering and expressing the truth of who I am. I am aware that life is supporting me and is for me. I am aware that everything happening is unfolding in divine, natural order and harmony. I know in my heart that every person I encounter and every relationship I have—be it for a minute, a decade, or a lifetime—is sacred and is perfectly designed for my expansion and experience. I am willing to see myself and others through the clear lens of Love, and I see my life as a beautiful gift of unfoldment. I am willing to see obstacles as opportunities. I am willing to raise my awareness and invite learning into my experience in a beautiful and graceful way. I am inviting grace into my life so that it can flow through the lessons my Soul has intended for me. I am aware that I am always being guided by my Authentic Self.

I am aware that my Authentic Self is filled with wisdom. I know that by following the lead of my Highest Self—by following my joy and seeing through the clear lens of Love—I am on the path that will reveal my fullest realized potential in this life. I am in the flow of life when I am feeling inspired and alive. I recognize these feelings as the open pathway my Soul is inviting me on. I am following the flow of my joy. And as I do this, I am filled with a sense of wonderment and a sense of awe for the mystery that is unfolding before me. I am aware that in allowing myself to feel and express a sense of expansion—and in continuing to move toward people, experiences, and situations that invoke this feeling within me—I am aligning more fully with my Authentic Self. I am allowing my true self and allowing myself to bloom. My spiritual Being is guiding me along this pathway. I deeply trust this process, knowing the alignment I feel with my joy is the unfolding of my entelechy and my Authentic Self's integration of my highest potential into my personality.

I am willing to follow my attention to places that invite feelings of upliftment. I am willing to explore people, situations, and experiences that bring me joy, knowing that this is the divine design that my Soul signed up for in this life. I am aware that this is inspiring within me a rich and fulfilling experience in my life.

In Arthurian myths, the Holy Grail—the actual chalice itself—was hidden near the Avalon orchard. The chalice was rumored to be in the Red Springs Chalice Well, located at the foot of the Glastonbury Tor. The Chalice Well has had running water for over two thousand years, generously offering twenty-five thousand imperial gallons a day to its people and visiting pilgrims. Additionally, it was thought that these life-giving waters made the soil rich, which resulted in the constant regeneration of seeds that later blossomed into beautiful gardens and pregnant orchards, decorating the abundant land.

The apples growing in Avalon were both regular (of this world) and golden (otherworldly). All of the apples looked the same: red and delicious. That is, until a person achieved spiritual sight. This person, now referred to as a seer, was then able to understand the difference between ordinary and magical apples. After that, seers could then place golden apples into the Grail cup, transforming them into a magical elixir.

The promise to the initiate is that just a sip of this miraculous drink will allow her to experience wholeness, immortality, and full awareness of her Original Wisdom. In that instant, the initiate will then become god/goddess realized. The point to remember is that this process can only begin with the initiate's willingness to see herself and the world through a different lens. It begins when she seeds her experience with thoughts not of the "real" world. Once the initiate drinks from the Holy Grail chalice, she is then attuned to her divinity, becoming the goddess.

Chapter Five

Thoughts Seed Things

"The world as we have created it is a process of our thinking.
It cannot be changed without changing our thinking."

~ Albert Einstein

In 1984, I was seventeen, and I saw a picture of a Chinese Shar Pei puppy-dog. I went bananas. I fell head over heels in love with these dogs. I thought about these damn dogs morning, noon, and night, and I was on a mission to figure out how to get one. A Chinese Shar Pei puppy was around $1200; they were not cheap. I was a kid in high school, so I didn't have any money. And if I did have that money, my parents surely wouldn't have allowed me to use it to get a family dog.

Keep in mind that this was long before the worldwide web existed, but my desire was strong enough that I managed to get my hands on pictures, news clippings, and advertisements of Chinese Shar Peis. I had images pinned on a corkboard, and every single day I checked the classifieds to see if someone was going to give me the chance to acquire one of these dogs with the $50 bucks I had saved up for this venture.

This obsession continued for months.

I placed *a lot* of energy into imagining what it would be like to have one of these wrinkly puppies to snuggle in my bed! What I also want to emphasize here is that I *100 percent believed* that I would find someone who would sell me one of these dogs for the amount of money I had. I just knew it. Months passed, and slowly, over time, I relaxed my grip and let my dream float further out of my awareness.

Months later, I was on the phone with a friend, and he said to me, "Hey, my sister's boyfriend is trying to find a home for a stray dog. Do you know anyone who wants a dog?"

I immediately said, "No," and didn't ask another single question.

We finished our conversation, and before we hung up he said to me again, "Okay, well remember to call me if you run into anyone who wants a Sharp *Pee*."

I froze.

"What? What did you say?"

He responded, "The Sharp *Pee*. The dog I was telling you about."

I sheepishly asked, "Do you mean a Shar *Pei*?"

"Yeah, I guess," he replied.

I brought her home a couple of days later. Her name was Jaba, and she became the family dog. I cuddled her every day. I loved that dog. Oh, and the cost? Zero. Nada. Nothing. She was just looking to be connected with loving people in a loving home.

I share this story with you as a demonstration of how you can literally bring something into your awareness through the energy of excitement and positive emotions. The thoughts in your head and your belief (claimed as true) that it is just a matter of time until you get what you're envisioning allow you to get what you want. Keep reading, and I will explain this to you. Your thoughts are seeded with energy, and that energy is intelligent. Bringing your conscious awareness to your thoughts in an intentional way is how you can begin to influence the experiences you are having in life.

Seeding What You Would Love

The Universe is a field of unlimited possibilities, and it is waiting to see what kind of seed you drop into it. Later in my life, when I still didn't have a full understanding of the mechanics of this universal law, I intentionally used my powers of manifestation to produce a $5,000, white, slipcovered couch, and I only paid $75 for it. This was a deliberate process, and at the time I didn't realize how specificity is incredibly important when you are asking the Universe to bring you something that you want to experience. The more specific you are, the easier it is for universal forces to organize things on our behalf.

I was really into shabby chic, and I fell in love with this designer named Rachel Ashwell. She had this incredible white, slipcovered couch that I drooled over. It was made with a white, cotton linen that was incredibly soft, and the cushions on this couch made you feel like you were being held in a cloud. I stopped in my tracks when I first saw one (yes, I realize it was only a couch). I loved it, and in that moment I decided it would be mine. The challenge? That couch was $5,000. To me, that was an enormous amount of money for a couch. Way more than what I could or was willing to spend. But in the same way I looked through the classified ads for a Chinese Shar Pei in 1984, I went to work canvasing the internet for couches similar to this couch.

Well, I discovered that Pottery Barn had a similar model. But that couch was $2,500, which was still quite a bit more than what I was in a position to spend. So, I modified my expectations and began searching for the exact name, style, make, and model of this couch. I was patient but focused. During nights and week-ends, I would just search.

Now, here is part of the second part of the secret recipe: I *believed* that I would find the couch. *It was only a matter of time,* I thought. I was determined to be patient, *knowing* that eventually the Universe would set up a meeting between me and this couch. And I didn't really care if it actually ever happened! Yet I never had a doubt. After all, at seventeen, I was able to get Jaba, a $1500 specialty-breed dog, for free. A couch? Easy! Honestly, I don't remember how long it took, but one day I found it on Craigslist. A woman in Newport Beach wanted it out of her beautiful home so that she could get a new couch. She listed it for $75. I rented a U-Haul, found someone to drive it, and went and fetched the couch. Done. It was perfect and practically free.

An important note here: Two critical components of intentional manifestation are to be *really* specific and to "remain open" to what the Universe has in store for you. In other words, relax your own rigid expectations for *how* you will co-create what you want with the Universe. It is important to approach what you want with an open mind and *remain unattached*. This, in my experience, is important because you often receive something a thousand times better than anything you were able to dream up on your own.

For example, let's talk about my manifestation of my husband. One night, I put on some Zen music, lit a candle, went into a meditative state, and wrote a list of the qualities I was looking for in my perfect mate. There were some crazy things on that list. For example, he had to have ties to the East Coast (where my family was from), and he had to be poetic and creative and also earn a good living. When I met Paul on Match, he was working as a real estate agent and creating oil paintings on the side as a hobby. His son lived in Long Island, New York, with his ex-wife. The story of this romance and magic is a whole other book, and I wanted to illustrate that anything is possible!

Before I learned about energy and the malleability of it, I would have told you that I was able to bring things about in my life through tenacity and will. While there may be some truth in that, I am also aware of the "efforting" that accompanies those two qualities. With true, intentional co-creation with universal forces, I still take action, and there is much more grace and ease. I am in the flow, and I trust that what the Universe is bringing my way is for the highest good of all and is something even better than what I might have imagined on my own.

Once I began understanding the universal principle of the Law of Magnetic Attraction, I realized this was a superpower I had always had but just hadn't acknowledged. I want to unfold it further so that you have the same confidence in your own abilities. Having a greater understanding of how the principle works is super helpful. Come on, this is going to be empowering. Indulge me.

Dreaming Up a Dream or a Drama

If everything is energy, then so are your thoughts. If you intend to change your life, you first need to change your thinking. I learned this over time, and I'm sharing with you the ideas and concepts that assisted me in changing my own thinking. This is not an easy task, and it may take some focus and work, and you can absolutely do it.

The progression of your thoughts is like the grooves in a record or the code in a computer. Your thinking is like a computer program in that it gets installed in your local mind and you live your life according to what the program says. If we're comparing it to a record, your thinking is like grooves that are deep and strong. They are foundational in the support of the patterns (programs) you are running. According to the National Science Foundation, an average person has about twelve thousand to sixty thousand thoughts per day. Of those, 80 percent are negative, and 95 percent are repetitive. They just repeat! You are a computer on autopilot. And you have the same programs (patterns) that run and rerun and rerun over and over and over again. Transforming these patterns is another great learning opportunity on the path of the Soul's journey.

Let's consider the following: What you think about expands. This means, as you give energy and emotion to your thoughts, they grow. When I invited that Shar Pei into my life, I had *a lot* of energy around that. It was the determined will of a headstrong teenager that co-created Jaba with the Universe. I want to illustrate the investment I made with my energy; it was in the form of the focus and attention I placed on getting myself one of these dogs.

When you give something your attention, you place your energy—your Life Force—into that something. Your emotions are energy in motion. When you give energy to something, you are literally fueling it, thus giving it a much higher probability of actually happening. The most important part of the energy lesson is that you need to place your attention, and therefore your energy, on what you *do* want to have occur in your life, not on what you *don't* want.

Because you are a multidimensional, energetic Being, you are a powerful creator. It takes no more energy to dream up a dream than it does to dream up a drama. Admit it. When something doesn't go your way, in about thirty seconds you can dream up all the things that could go wrong or will go wrong. You can quickly convince yourself that what you want won't work out, and so on. Why don't you use your imagination for what you do want? We've all had the experience of multiple "negative" experiences happening at once. Admittedly, when this occurs, it's easier to conclude it's all going downhill, and the truth is that you do have a choice. Consider your "long line" of negative creations as a confirmation that you are powerful. What? Yes, you're powerful; you are creating what you are thinking about. The problem is that when you are focusing on "negative possibilities," that is what you experience. Another possibility is, what if what you perceive as "negative" is really a gift in disguise? What if the Universe is giving you a cue that "this door is closed" to you for a reason?

You can create your life through conscious intention or blatant disregard. When you are sick, it's easier to focus on the illness than it is to intentionally focus on health. Either way, your life will be created. I am inviting you to play a more participatory role in what is being created by intentionally directing your thoughts, emotions, and actions toward what it is you *want* to experience. To consciously create your life, it requires conscious intention.

The disclaimer here is that regardless of what you want to create, you life will be in support of your Earth school lessons. What does this mean? You and I, and *all* humans, are here to learn about love and to reconnect with our Original Wisdoms. And each of us has our own Soul's purpose (our own entelechy). That is the real reason we are here.

Aside from that, you have *a lot* of choice. Do you want a specialty dog? Do you want an expensive white couch? Do you want a spouse who is financially secure and creative, and who has East Coast ties? Life will help you create *anything* you put your intention on. The truth is, the really important thing is not *what* you create (the dogs, the couches, our relationships); rather, what's important is who you are and *what unfolds inside of you as you learn that you can create*. (And I'm getting ahead of myself here.)

One other really important note: If your Soul signed you up in this life for your fullest expression as an apple, there is nothing that's going to make you an orange. And this is why it's critically important you discover what is true *inside* of you. If you're an apple, Love being the expression of the apple.

Until you are fully aware of the powers you have as a creator, it's easy to constantly "miscreate" your life. Your thoughts are like seeds, and your emotions are like water; your emotions help your thoughts to grow. It's your choice whether you feed your thoughts with the energy of Love or fear. E-motion is energy-in-motion. Dr. Joe Dispenza said, "It is our feelings that literally 'matter' or give substance to our thoughts."

The Illumination of Miscreation

I define "miscreation" as *the unintentional direction of Life Force energy that produces an unfavorable outcome. This is the result of emitting an unsupportive frequency that is then matched through the Law of Magnetic Attraction.* We have all experienced such "miscreations." I also know now that each of these "miscreations" were beautifully designed opportunities for my learning and expansion. But at the time, let's face it, it can feel like hell.

I've already mentioned my frozen shoulder, but let me unfold the whole drama for you. At the moment I first sat down in the USM classroom on that fateful October Friday night in 2013, I noticed the odd and painful stabbing in my right shoulder. I remember rubbing it and thinking, *Wow, this is really painful. I wonder what is going on.* It bothered me for the entire weekend. I ignored this pain for about a year, until I literally could not lift my arm above my breast. It turned out that I had adhesive capsulitis, otherwise known as a frozen shoulder. Throughout the process of ignoring some clear information my body was communicating to me, I did try a lot of physical therapy, holistic treatments, energy healing, and massages, along with a truckload of topical tiger balms. And as I was doing all of these things, I was mad. This *problem* was interrupting my life. I didn't have time for this! After all, I was working sixty hours a week *and* pursuing a master's degree. Notice where my attention was: Ignoring a problem and being angry about it. This became the energetic signature I was a match for.

All I did was complain about it. In a way, I was looking for attention and sympathy. I felt and thought about the pain a lot. I perpetuated it by going around telling everyone about just how much agony I was in. I miscreated my life through this experience by making sure I was telling everyone (on a regular basis, mind you) about how terrible I felt, how my body ached, and how I never felt rested. I complained about using pharmaceuticals for all of my ailments, as they were just one big Band-Aid. I would complain about and share this story with anyone who would listen. I would go so far as to demonstrate for them, saying, "Look, I can only lift my arm to here," as I winced, straining to lift my limb the best I could.

This *became* my story. For about a year.

Until that day on the plane. If you've not connected this dot yet, let me reiterate: *You are a creator.* Think back to what you learned in chapter one. You are an individualized expression of the Divine. This infinitely intelligent energy is the composition of who you are.

I say to my clients all the time, "Use your powers for good." Thoughts are things. Living, breathing things. Things like seeds. Your thoughts are how you "place your order" with the Universe. Your thoughts are the energy before the matter. Everything in your Universe is first a thought. Nothing can exist unless someone first thought it up. Vision, or visualization, is the energetic template or blueprint that commands molecules. Today's thoughts are quite literally creating your future. As Albert Einstein said, "Your imagination is the preview to life's coming attractions." You've probably heard it before, and I will share it again: "You are the creator of your own reality." Your attention is how the Universe knows what you want.

Are you really taking this in? Are you ready now to actually take action and direct your thoughts with more precision and intention? Are you ready to pay a greater level of attention to what you are investing your Life Force energy in? *If you want a different life, you must change the energy you're giving out.* In other words, the story you are telling. To change the story you're telling, you have to change where you place your attention. What would happen if you began to tell the story of what you *want* to experience? What would it take for you to more fully own that your thoughts are the communication link between the physical world and the Infinite Intelligence powering the Universe?

Esther Hicks, an incredible channel for the teachings of Abraham (a non-physical, collective consciousness), shares that molecules begin to organize and rearrange themselves when a thought or feeling is held for as little as seventeen seconds. Being conscious and deliberate about your thoughts is how you create your experience. Esther shares that if we can hold our attention, without resistance, on a thought and corresponding feeling for seventeen seconds, we begin to manifest from that point of attraction. When focusing for sixty-eight seconds, it then puts energy into motion, to the extent that it will likely manifest into your physical world. Can you hold the vision for what you would love to experience for sixty-eight seconds?

If you want more information on this science, check out Dr. Joe Dispenza (from chapter two) and his many books. He founded a methodology that supports the idea that there is an incredibly strong bridge between science and spirituality.

Why Is It So Hard to Let Go of Negative Thoughts?

There are many reasons why you might have trouble releasing your negative thoughts. One is habit. You are simply so used to focusing your attention on negative thoughts that you have to work to notice when you do this, and you have to be conscious of changing your negative thoughts into positive ones. You also crave social acknowledgement of your trials. You want people to commiserate with you. You are not alone. We all do this. We are human! Here's the thing: Negative thoughts cause stress, and stress produces a chemical cocktail in your physiology. This happens in the form of the hormone cortisol. Negative thoughts weaken your ability to create from a place of possibility.

Ralph Waldo Emmerson said, "Stand guard at the portal of your mind." Pay attention to what is happening in there. Be the observer of your own mind. Catch yourself when you are having an unsupportive thought pattern and disrupt it! One way to disrupt your thought patterns is by moving your energy. Get up, dance, sing, walk, or run. I've heard Mary Morrissey make this suggestion when talking about interrupting negative thoughts; she says to firmly slap your hand on the table and make this declaration out loud: "I interrupt this broadcast!"

What is one way you can interrupt yourself the next time you find yourself caught in a negative loop?

Imagining Your Life into Form

Just as I was able to materialize a Shar Pei, a beautiful white couch, and even my husband, you, too, can use the energetic power of your thoughts to more intentionally create what you want in life. Your thoughts and emotions are emitting energy out into the Universe. Through the Law of Magnetic Attraction, the energy we put out will magnetize to its own match. Being mindful about what you envision—so that you invest your Life Force energy in what you want instead of constricting your true desires with fearful, negative thoughts—will only assist you in getting what you want. The intention is to create, not miscreate. I'm not suggesting this is a direct response game. If you think of an elephant crashing through your house, it doesn't happen. It's a fleeting thought. Ridiculous. I am, however, suggesting that you influence what you do and do not experience depending on where you place your attention. If you have limiting beliefs that interfere with your ability to envision the life you want to experience, hang tight, as we will be addressing that in the next chapter.

When I was younger, I wanted puppies and fancy couches. Today, I am much more interested in peace, joy, cooperation, harmony, and feeling alive. The principle is the same. When you focus on peace, see peace, and look for peace, you'll find peace and be peace. When you focus on peace, you have a much better chance of flooding your experience with peace. Don't take my word for it, however. Give it a try and see what happens.

In the next chapter, we'll take this a step further by exploring how your thoughts can form into an entire belief system that shapes your experience.

Opportunity for Transformation
Take Action

This is the fifth Opportunity for Transformation. This is your chance to take action and move your life forward, discover a new part of your consciousness, and create an experience for yourself that will deepen your learning of this material. All of the OFTs are designed to assist you in more fully integrating Original Wisdom from your Authentic Self into your day-to-day life. If you would like to download an actual worksheet or listen to an audio version of this OFT, please visit donnabond.com/opportunityfortransformation.

Illuminate Your "Miscreations"

As a reminder, the definition of a miscreation is the unintentional direction of Life Force energy that produces an unfavorable outcome. This is a result of emitting an unsupportive frequency that is then matched through the Law of Magnetic Attraction.

Are you willing to get honest with yourself right now and bring some real truth into your awareness? If you are willing, this exercise can produce some profound realizations and will increase self-awareness in your life.

Are you willing to identify the thoughts you're having and stories you're telling yourself that are unsupportive of the experience you want to have in your life? What are the big thoughts? Name two or three "storylines" that you continue to tell yourself and others regarding "how hard you have it." What are the repetitive thoughts clinking around in your mind, and perhaps playing out in your life, that you might consider "miscreations." One of my examples was a frozen shoulder.

Here is a list of inner inquiries that will assist you in revealing your miscreations. Grab your journal and your favorite pen.

1. Is there an unfavorable situation in your life that you give a lot of attention and focus to? If so, what is it?

2. Is there a situation that you feel is out of your control, yet you still find yourself obsessing over the circumstances, wishing they were different?

3. Is there a relationship in your life that is filled with discontent? Do you find yourself constantly thinking about how this person has "wronged you?" Do you continue to fuel the situation with anger and resentment?

4. Is there a health challenge in your life that you are consumed with mentally, physically, emotionally, and financially? How are you relating to this situa-

tion? Do you find yourself ignited with the energy of anger or unfairness, or are you perhaps just annoyed that you are too busy to really "deal with" the situation?

5. Is there anything happening in your life—something that you find you give an incredible amount of energy and focus to—that is just not working the way you want it to?

Be gentle with yourself here. Even a little shift toward your willingness to see these situations, can support you in stepping yourself onto a new path of possibility.

Sacred Truth Activation

This is the fifth Sacred Truth Activation. Find a quiet, private space to center yourself, light a candle, and speak these words aloud. If you would like to listen to an audio version of this guided personal decree, please visit donnabond.com/sacredtruthactivations.

I Am the Power of My Thoughts

I am aware of the power of my thoughts. I am repatterning old cycles of limitation by shifting my energetic attention, and thus my energy, onto what I do want to experience. I am aware that consciously placing my energy—my Life Force—as the formulation of my thoughts, is how I use my power as a creator to influence the organizing principle of the Universe to collaborate on my behalf. I am aware that wherever I place my attention, the Universe will begin to find a match to that, fulfilling the Law of Magnetic Attraction and aligning with the vibration that I am offering. I am using my powers of creation with my thoughts. I am giving my attention to what I want to experience in life.

I am aware that if something comes into my experience that I do not prefer, I can choose to redirect my thought or reframe the situation so that I can see it as the beautifully designed life lesson that it is. I am aware that my Higher Self has given me this particular experience for a reason. I am in alignment with placing my attention on the growth available to me in every situation as it's happening. I am also aware that I can choose to change a thought that isn't supportive to the way I want to live. I can change my mind and my focus at any time.

I am aware that I am a creator. I am able to direct my energy, and thus my precious Life Force, toward situations I want to experience. I empower myself and enliven my Spirit as I align with this idea.

Many linear-brained, analytical fact-checkers may say that the legend of Avalon is only a myth. Our goddess, now awakened after the sip of the magic elixir, suggests that everything is reflected in the way one sees things. Over and over again, we have all been invited to the land of imaginative thinking. Invited to believe in unlimited possibility, infinite potential, or perhaps the confinement of dungeons and dragons that are lurking around each corner. Each engagement with life, of course, invites the challenge of moving oneself from the known to the unknown, where dragons show themselves, inviting our growth or defeat.

The goddess's thoughts and beliefs directly affect the experience she will have. She maintains the power to believe in her own truth. When she learns to honor her unique, divine expression along the way, she eventually discovers she has always been fully equipped with everything she needs for the journey. It is then that miracles begin to materialize. With this perspective, she shapes her world in many magical ways. She is the only one who essentially believes that life's adventure can be either ordinary or miraculous.

Chapter Six

Your Beliefs Create Your World

"Whether you think you can, or you
think you can't—you're right."

~ Henry Ford

I am the daughter of second-generation immigrants. On both sides of my family, my parents' parents came over "on the boat," as we say. My grandparents believed that life was about hard work and sacrifice, and they instilled this belief in my parents, and my parents instilled it in me. This was how I ended up with a whole lot of money and prestige as well as a frozen shoulder.

I also grew up believing I wasn't very smart. As a result, I pushed myself and felt like I had to prove myself again and again. I bought into the idea that everyone else (parents, teachers, friends, media, and so on) *knew better than me.*

I call bullshit.

You have the choice of taking personal responsibility for your thoughts. What beliefs were you taught? Is there a different way to think? Is there a way that is more supportive of the experience you want to have? Are you willing to consider another way, a different perspective, a different point of view? Do the feelings you are aware of *inside yourself* align with (or conflict with) what you're seeing *outside* yourself?

Let me call your attention to when people thought the world was flat or when they believed it was impossible to put a man on the moon. These are old, outdated belief systems. Had people not been willing to expand beyond these stagnant ideas, they would not have grown. We would not have evolved as humanity.

One of the beliefs that really serves my life is the belief that *everyone* is simply doing the best they can at the time, using the belief systems they have and the tools they're working with. If you go through your life blaming your parents, your teachers, society, the government, and this, and this, and… You catch my drift. We all base our decision-making on the ideas and beliefs we were taught. However, we get to decide, individually, if we want to introduce something new into our lives or if we want to remain stuck in the old loop. This is a pivotal choice you have in your life. Are you willing to let in something new? Are you willing to examine the programs you've been given and the patterns you've developed? Are you willing to embrace the part of your life's learning journey that is the deconstruction of those beliefs and the rebuilding of your life in a more loving and supportive way?

Of course, the ideal intention is to create your life in cooperation with universal law and loving. At the highest level of consciousness, you are Love. When you live from this place of loving, residing in loving, you naturally make choices that are for the highest good of all concerned.

Can Being Hardheaded Be a Good Thing?

Though I've had the misbelief that "I'm not that smart," encoded within my personality is a willful, headstrong drive. This was operating regardless of what other people thought. As a result, I've been accused of being impractical, illogical, quick to react without thinking, and (likely from my parents) just plain stupid.

In 2013, my husband and I found a beautiful home in Southern California that we fell in love with. We made an offer on it and put my condo up for sale so that we could finance a mortgage for the new property. I had a number in my head that I *believed* I could get for my condo. I had bought the real estate at the top of the market in 2006, and my equity was gone. The price in my mind would just cover the outstanding debt on the current mortgage. *No one*, aside from me, believed I could get the price I was asking. Not my husband (a former realtor), not our current realtor, and, most convincingly, not the market conditions. And because I'm "hardheaded," I insisted on this price and wasn't going to be talked out of it. Honestly, I wasn't trying to be difficult or tricky. I was told repeatedly that I was risking losing our dream house if we couldn't sell the condo. And I remained confident about the price I had in my head and offered my long rebuttal list about why I believed we would get that price.

First of all, my condo was super cute! And based on all the other condos in the development, it was one of only three places that had a driveway that connected directly to the street. Whoever bought it wouldn't have to drive into the development to get home. It featured one brick wall and had exposed ceiling beams. The kitchen was open, and the sun streamed into all the right places at certain times of the day. The sweet little patio overlooked the entire complex perched above the entire development.

I had my reasons, and deep in my core I truly believed I could get my price. Everyone gave into my stubbornness, and they threw up their hands, though they believed I was just wasting my time. I wasn't. In twenty-four hours, I received three full-price offers on the condo. Did you catch that? THREE! One of the offers was cash, eliminating the need for an appraisal and making the market conditions irrelevant. We had not yet heard back on the offer we had made to the sellers of our dream home, but we took the risk and sold the condo out from underneath us, and I got to gloat for the rest of the weekend.

The sellers returned their counter a few days into the week, denying our offer due to the original contingency we had made to sell the condo. We removed the contingency, countered again, and got the house!

So, what did I learn through all of this? That I am stubborn and hardheaded? Some would say yes. And here is what I know: I truly *believed* that I could get the price I was asking for. I had my list of reasons, and while logic was not on my side, I still believed in my core that it was possible. I attribute my success to my belief and my intuition.

What Do You Want to Believe?

As a child, you were taught (in my house, you were *told)* what to believe. Your parents and teachers instructed you based on their own experiences as well as on what they knew and what they believed. (I want to point out that my parents and teachers were doing the best they could with what they had to work with, and so were yours. So, cut them some slack now.) You get to redefine your beliefs for the continuation of evolution, and you can shape the world into what you want it to look like. I also want to encourage you to be gentle and compassionate with yourself as you work through this chapter, confronting all of the things you've been taught to believe that are not supporting you and your life right now. Sometimes people can get really upset with themselves for not questioning these beliefs earlier, or they can get really upset with their parents, teachers, and society for passing these "rules" down to them. I encourage you to be as kind and gentle with yourself as possible. What if your Soul's plan was to come to this life to specifically evolve certain beliefs?

You get to decide what you want to believe. I hear some of you saying, "Well, there is the truth and the opposite of the truth. There is right, and there is wrong." I want to be the voice that poses the questions, "What is true inside of *you*? What do *you* want to believe? What rings true in *your* core?" And, equally important, "What does *not* ring true?" Whatever you believe will have a direct correlation with the experiences you have in your life.

As our collective consciousness evolves, we have been invited into the idea that *anything* is possible. We have all literally been stretched beyond our current belief systems and sent into the realm that teaches us that, really, anything is possible. As you invite more possibilities into your experience, can you consider that you get to believe anything you want? If your beliefs were different, how might your life be different?

Shifting Limiting Beliefs
Leads to Personal Transformation

The belief system and paradigms inside of you shape your experience and your reality. Regardless of whether they are expansive or limiting, your beliefs dictate your life experience. Your beliefs and paradigms were shaped by your experiences, your interactions with the adults and peers in your life, and the religion and society you were raised in. Among other things.

You live your life according to your own thoughts and beliefs. You limit your life in profound ways when you stay confined by limiting beliefs. There is a story about a guy who is fishing; he throws back most of the fish he catches after measuring them with a ruler. When asked why he keeps tossing back the big fish he keeps catching, he says, "My frying pan is only eight inches long." This is a wonderful metaphor for how you can dismiss possibility in your life because it does not conform to the belief system you have.

When your beliefs allow you to be open to the unlimited possibilities in the world, truly anything can happen. Identifying and changing your limiting beliefs is the single most important step you can take to improve your life. You may not even realize that you're living according to beliefs that may or may not be true for you. You take on ideas, concepts, ways of being, and rules that have been handed down to you from others.

The beliefs you adopt create your reality. If you have a core belief that you will never be good with money, for example, you will never be good with money. If you are so set in your beliefs that you are unwilling to look at them, you will never be able to evolve them, and you will remain stuck because you've locked yourself into a life where you're confined by your beliefs. Just by believing something is possible for you, you immediately shift your perspective, and the probability of that event actually happening for you is higher. If you believe it will never be possible, I can assure you that then is the truth.

As I mentioned earlier, my father died at the young age of forty-four. He was a workaholic. He followed in his father's footsteps, and for a while I followed in his. And this is how it happens: the cycle repeats. I grew up believing that my self-worth was directly related to how hard I worked. I grew up "conditioned" to believe that in order to *earn* love, attention, and worthiness, I had to work hard. I had to prove myself to others to be accepted and to be considered a "good person." Also operating in my subconscious was the notion that I had to succeed through hard work and sacrifice. Because of that, my learned pattern of being a workaholic started outwardly manifesting its miscreation and misalignment in the form of physical, mental, emotional, and spiritual discontent.

Your beliefs create your world. Limiting beliefs are operating in your subconscious all the time. For transformation to occur, you must identify these beliefs, excavate them, shine the light on them, and decide if they *are* true for you and if you want to keep them. Living inside a box is optional.

Learning from Your Old Belief System

Spiritually speaking, it's not an accident that you grew up with the belief system you had. When you remember that the higher part of you—your unlimited Self—likely knows exactly what is happening and is aware of the learning opportunities being offered to you, you can trust that you've inherited a particular belief system for a reason. On a Soul level, you essentially "opted in" on the belief system you have. This is because the Soul is looking for things that challenge and conflict with the true you. Everything you experience in life supports your growth and evolution, including all of the challenges and hardships you face.

I know a family that is steadfast in the beliefs of their organized construct. Their daughter, who gave me permission to share this with you, had a son. That child, at the age of five, said, "Mom, my Soul is a girl." I'm pretty sure their religion does not accept or approve of this. Regardless, this incredible mom supports and honors her child's true identity. She has her kid in counseling and attends parent support groups. She helps her child transition into her life as a young lady, not a young lad. I imagine that the grandparents' belief systems did not support this idea, but all I see are open hearts and accepting minds. What is most present in this story is love. Everyone loves this little kid—the parents, the grandparents, and all who were able to move beyond their old belief systems. Because they love this little girl so much, they, along with their family and friends, have been given a precious and sacred opportunity to reshape their beliefs and further evolution. What a miracle!

This is how your life invites you to reestablish new paradigms. This is how evolution occurs. Changing your beliefs requires trust in a Higher Power. Life asks that you open yourself up to a different, more uplifting, joy-filled way of seeing things in your life. When you can trust that there is a learning opportunity available to you in every challenging (Soul lesson) situation you face, through the process of transformation, there is a gift waiting to be revealed. Once you decide that you have a true desire to evolve your life experience, you will then be willing to begin the process of examining your beliefs.

When you hold tightly to what you have believed in the past, you only get more of the same. This is why opening yourself up to new possibilities is a pivotal point in transforming your limiting beliefs. It is only through the process of the unfolding of your life that you grow into the fullest realized expression of yourself. It's empowering to know you are able to transform anything that's out of alignment with your true self.

There is a universal limiting belief that says that when things are not happening the way you think they should be happening, things are not happening the "right" way. On a deeper level, this universal limiting belief says that you don't believe the way things are happening is perfect. In other words, you don't believe in the divine perfection of the Universe. If you really believe in a Higher Power—an Infinite Intelligence or God—then where is your faith that things are unfolding the way they are for a reason? Even when you don't like something, or when you believe something is "wrong." From a scientific standpoint, if the planets were just slightly "off" from their current positions, our entire Universe would self-combust. I always think of this when I'm bringing myself into alignment and realizing that things are happening perfectly. If they were not, we probably wouldn't be here at all.

When the sequence of things do not take you in the direction you want to go in, you have a tendency to label it as "wrong." Can you consider that this Infinite Intelligence, of which we are a part, is smarter than your "learned" self? Remember, your Soul has much more wisdom, guidance, and knowledge for you and your life than the patterned, programmed, small-self mind does. Can you consider that your Soul (and let's say God, for that matter) has a grander plan that is unfolding for your benefit? Though you can't see the whole picture considering the narrow scope of your ego, it doesn't mean it's not unfolding for a reason you might not be aware of. Is it possible that things are evolving in a way that is *even better* than anything you could have imagined?

To begin to shift your old beliefs, you must resist viewing your life from a narrow perspective. There is a larger, greater plan than what is evident to your ego-based self. If you're lucky, your logical, local mind will get a glimmer of the multidimensionality that is you.

An individual learning opportunity occurs when you shift from the belief that "things are going wrong" to the belief that "things are happening in alignment with each Soul's plan, even if I can't see what that is right now." You'll also know your beliefs are shifting if you find yourself thinking, "If something is unfolding for me that I'm not pleased with, perhaps it means that this is what it looks like while it's getting worked out. All is well." You probably get upset when you don't get the job, when there is no call following the date, or when your dream house is sold to someone else. However, can you consider that life is doing you a big favor? Poet, truth-teller, and love-devotee Hollie Holden calls this a "cosmic redirection." When you don't get your way, is it possible to just relax, knowing that it's all perfect the way it is going? You have the opportunity to learn that just because it's not going "your way," it doesn't mean it's going the "wrong way."

When you are having an experience you don't like or don't want, ask yourself the following questions: "What is here for me? What can I be learning from this circumstance or situation? What is my Soul inviting me to learn, to become aware of, to notice?" What would be different in your life if you believed that everything was unfolding perfectly?

The discontent I experienced in my former career, the health crises that removed me from the old mechanical life I was sleeping through, the advice of a psychic to pursue a master's in a field I had no experience in at the time, my dad cutting down my apple tree and then dying when I was only twenty-two—I can now see that all of this is perfect. It all happened for a purpose. It all unfolded with precision and perfection, leading me to where I am today. What if, while going through life, I had believed in the grander plan and recognized that it was *all* exactly as it is meant to be? Do you agree that I would have saved myself a generous amount of heartache and emotional pain?

What if you believed everything in your life was in divine order and was being presented to you in that specific way for a reason? What if everything was exactly as it was meant to be? Everything.

Believe What You Want to Believe

As you now know, your beliefs have a powerful effect on your life, so it's important to examine your limiting beliefs and update them with positive, supportive beliefs. You *are* enough. You *can* find happiness, love, and success. Your dreams *are* possible. You *do* have the time and motivation. You're capable enough and resourceful enough to generate the money. You *don't* have to struggle. And you *don't* need others' approval to be *you*. Trust your intuition. When you believe that something is possible—whether that's selling your house, finding a new job, or meeting your soulmate—it is possible.

What do you want to believe? Remember, you get to choose what you believe about something. You can't change the circumstances of the world, but you can change the way you think about them. The result of shifting your beliefs is extraordinary personal transformation. Look at the areas where you struggle in life and identify the beliefs that are supporting those struggles. Choose to see these challenges as learning opportunities from your Soul. What do you need to believe in order to have a different experience? Can you believe that it's not all on you? Are you willing to believe that everything is getting handled perfectly in your life? That your Soul is guiding you and that God's got it? How would your life experience be different if this were your new belief?

In the next chapter, you'll learn to distinguish between the repetitive voice of your ego and the wisdom of your Authentic Self.

Opportunity for Transformation
Take Action

This is the sixth Opportunity for Transformation. This is your chance to take action and move your life forward, discover a new part of your consciousness, and create an experience for yourself that will deepen your learning of this material. All of the OFTs are designed to assist you in more fully integrating Original Wisdom from your Authentic Self into your day-to-day life. If you would like to download an actual worksheet or listen to an audio version of this OFT, please visit donnabond.com/opportunityfortransformation.

Identify Limiting Beliefs

Before you can invite yourself to consider a new direction, you must first come to terms with where you are now. This is where you have the opportunity to become really clear about some of the limiting beliefs that are operating in your consciousness. Once you are willing to *be* where you are in the present, you can start moving in the direction you want to *go* toward.

Below is a list of limiting beliefs. By no means is this exhaustive. Limiting beliefs are varied and plentiful. Before you look at this list, get a pen and a notebook. Maybe light a candle. Close your eyes and ask to connect to that higher, multidimensional aspect of your true essence. When you're ready, ask, "What are the limiting beliefs I am currently holding that are preventing me from living into the full potential of my life?" See what comes forward. Jot it down. Be with it. Resist the urge to judge it or make it wrong. *This is simply a process of noticing.* This is an exercise in awareness, of shining the light on what is ready to be seen. In this moment, you are not changing anything; you are just tuning into where you are. After a while, if you need some assistance, take a look at the list of limiting beliefs. Write down anything that feels activated or true inside you.

Limiting Belief Exercise:
Get a highlighter. Review this list quickly and highlight the beliefs that are operating in your life. Don't overthink it.

Go.

- The more money I have, the more people will like me.
- The more money I have, the happier I'll be.
- I must prove myself to earn respect from others.

- I must prove myself to show my value and worth to the world.
- The more material success I have, the happier I will be.
- If everyone likes me, I will have a better life.
- What I do or achieve in life dictates my value and worth.
- What other people think of me defines who I am.
- I need others' approval to feel I'm making the right choice.
- I rely more on logic and empirical data than on my own gut feelings when I make decisions in my life.
- It's not okay to be vulnerable or to allow my real emotions to surface.
- Being positive all the time is the only recipe for success.
- Other people know better than me.
- If I'm going to experience any success or achievement in life, I must do something to make it happen.
- Connecting heart to heart with other people is way too scary and vulnerable.
- If I'm happy while others are suffering, it means I don't care.
- I can't be my true self, or I will be judged.
- I will be happy when _____.
- If they really loved me, they would _____.
- If I find love, it will only lead to a broken heart.
- If I speak my truth, I will be rejected.
- I'm a bad/unlovable person.
- I can't pursue my dreams because they aren't important.

- I can't pursue my dreams because there's no time to do it and there's no money in it.
- No matter what I'm doing, I think I should be doing something else.
- I should be further along than I am.
- I should be there by now.
- Things never work out for me.
- I'll never make enough money.
- I'll always have to struggle, while others have it easier.
- Physical problems always keep me from happiness and success.
- I don't have the time or the space to get all mushy with my feelings.
- If people really get to know me, they won't like me.
- I am not _____ enough. (smart, talented, thin, attractive, educated, etc.)
- If I love myself, I am a narcissist.
- If I love myself, people will think I'm selfish.
- I can't do anything right.
- I must be perfect, or why bother?
- Everything is up to me.
- I need to go along with everyone else so I will be liked.
- If I dance to my own drum, I will lose the people I love.
- If I want to have a happy life, I need to control everything.
- I will get it done when _____.
- I will be happy when _____.

- I must keep up with the Joneses.
- I can only move forward if I have all the facts and know how it's going to turn out.
- I just can't do it.
- I am too old.
- I'll never be able to get out of this.
- If I am too happy and am not suffering, people won't love me.
- I have to earn love by doing things for others.

As an even deeper exercise, you can reword or reframe the limiting beliefs you identified. You can go back over the list and review what you have highlighted. This is where you can dive deep. Hold up the flashlight to each of these limiting beliefs and ask yourself the following questions:

1. If I call upon the wisdom and guidance of my Soul, will I still find that belief is true?

2. Am I willing to release and update this belief?

3. How can I transform this belief into a new belief that will support me in moving my life forward in a direction I want to go in?

4. What other beliefs hold this belief in place inside me?

5. Which of my behaviors and actions perpetuate this belief?

6. If I could wave a magic wand and make a new and improved belief to replace this one, what would it be?

For example, if you picked "I am too old" from the list above, you can change it to this: "I'm just the right age to do what I want to do. My years of experience qualify me to help others and make the positive difference I want to make."

Finding the Evidence to Support Your Updated Beliefs

As a way to support yourself in shifting over to your new beliefs, identify small things that prove your updated, reframed beliefs are true. Your thinking mind loves proof. This is a way you can help yourself get on board with your new, updated beliefs.

For example, let's say you have a limiting belief that you have to do things all on your own. Perhaps the story is that no one helps you, and you've bought into the idea that you have to do it all. An example of an updated belief could be this: "I am so supported by the Universe in every way." At first, this may seem awkward or flat-out incorrect. That's okay. This is how you could begin identifying "evidence" that you are receiving support: "I am supported by the chair I am sitting in right now, and that chair is supported by the floor it's sitting on. I am so supported by the clothes I am wearing, which protect my body from the cold and give me a feeling of security. I am so supported by the roof over my head." And so on and so forth. The more you can find ways to prove that your updated belief is true, the more you actually *embody the energetic vibrational signature that is a match to that*. When you embody the "match," the Law of Magnetic Attraction works on your behalf and creates more supportive experiences in your life.

Sacred Truth Activation

This is the sixth Sacred Truth Activation. Find a quiet, private space to center yourself, light a candle, and speak these words aloud. If you would like to listen to an audio version of this guided personal decree, please visit donnabond.com/sacredtruthactivations.

I Am Shaping My Life Through Beliefs

I am aware that my beliefs create my world. I am learning and exploring the belief system I was raised with, and I am aware that I can choose to update these beliefs in a way that is supportive of how I would like to experience my life. I am aware that when I see my life through the perspective of my Higher Self, or my Soul, I am seeing all of life with love, and I am aware that everything that is happening is presenting me with the opportunity to learn, grow, evolve, and expand. I am aware that many of my deeply engrained beliefs are the stepping stones for me to recreate new experiences in my life.

I am aware that the slightest shift in my beliefs can make a significant difference in my life experience. I am aware that I can relax when things do not seem to be going "my way." I am able to take a step back and remind myself that everything is happening to benefit me. I choose to update how I see the world. I change my beliefs to support the experience I want to have. I am aware that when I live my life in support of my expanded evolution, this creates a strong foundation in my life. I accept and allow more love, success, clarity, abundance, and fun to enter my life.

At 521 feet high, the Glastonbury Tor is a landmark that can be seen from miles. From the top of the conical hill, one has a 360-degree view and can see nearby Wells, the Quantocks, the Mendips, luscious peat moors leading out to sea, and, on a clear day, the brilliant Welsh mountains. Standing majestically at the top of the Tor is the fourteenth-century tower of St. Michael, who is honored as an advocate and protector of the Divine.

From the highest point on the Isle of Avalon, the goddess receives significantly Higher Guidance than she does when standing at the bottom. This is a parallel to how her Higher Self sees more of the world than her limited, smaller Human Self. From up above, a higher, long-range perspective allows the goddess to see the aligned pathways ahead, which will help her avoid unnecessary obstacles and benefit from the most obscured shortcuts. The insufficiencies of the logical mind, which can be compared to the bottom of the mountain, are limited by short-sightedness. This small self is truly only able to rely on information it receives from the path it already traveled. And the past, in no way, can define the future.

Take note: When traveling the adventure with the full integration of both parts, success is eminent. Being connected with our Higher Self and tuned into our Human Self allows one to receive a built-in line of communication to our whole self with All That Is.

Chapter Seven

Higher Guidance

"The intuitive mind is a sacred gift and the rational mind is a faithful servant. We have created a society that honors the servant and has forgotten the gift."

~ Albert Einstein

Transcending the Hook

After I quit my corporate job and started working as a marketing consultant (still before I became a coach), I made numerous changes. I really slowed down. I started meditating every day, and I began eating healthy smoothies that I made in my Vitamix™. I started walking daily. I became more fully present and listened more to my inner guidance. My shoulder now had flexibility and moved with ease. My life as a solopreneur was beginning to gel. I was making great money, and I was only working about three days a week. This allowed me to concentrate on my studies as I pursued my master's at the University of Santa Monica.

Life was clicking along. Despite the massive changes I had already made, including coming down off the adrenaline of a sixty-hours-a-week job, the Universe had another important lesson in store for me. Regardless of my new, more relaxed environment while working for myself, in which I began each day with meditation and spiritual contemplation, I still had a great deal of learning to do about my addiction to *doing*. I attribute my landing on the path of "awakening" to my frozen shoulder. But what happened next was the Universe's way of making sure I was paying attention. An exclamation of sorts, it was also the reason I was able to significantly strengthen my inner superpower: my intuition.

It was the middle of March of 2015, and I was halfway through my second year at USM. I woke up rather abruptly one morning after a dream. In the dream, I was looking at myself in the mirror. I saw that a fishhook had punctured my left breast. It was bloody and messy. I could see that the barb and the sharp point had made it all the way through my fleshy breast. I looked up at myself in the mirror and said out loud, "How am I going to get out of this?" My voice was so clear and loud in the dream, the content so shocking, that it jolted me awake. I sat up in my bed, awake and alert. I replayed the dream in my mind and suddenly remembered a little grain of sand that I had felt on my breast about six weeks earlier. I wondered, *Is that little grain of sand still there?* I felt my left breast. Indeed, it was.

I made an appointment that day, which eventually turned into several appointments. First the OBGYN, then the ultrasound, then the biopsy. After poking around in my breast with a needle, the last thing my radiologist said to me was, "I'm sure this is nothing, but we've gotta prove it." I left the biopsy office and literally didn't give it a second thought. I believed that guy when he said it was nothing. I didn't really tell anyone. I didn't talk about it and actually didn't even think about it.

Days later, I was being called back into "the little room" for my results. My husband had asked to be at the appointment, and as we were waiting together in the little room, it suddenly occurred to me that there was a problem. I flashed back to when doctors had told me my father was going to die. They take you into a little room when they give you bad news.

Just as I was feeling a rush of panic, in came the doctor I had seen before, the one who had said it was nothing. He was accompanied by a nurse coordinator. We all sat at this little table, looking at one another. The doctor asked, "How did you find this?" so I told him the story about my dream. He commended me for listening to my body and then proceeded to give me the diagnosis: triple-negative, stage-one breast cancer.

I was receiving this diagnosis five days before my forty-seventh birthday. I suddenly felt like an observer. Like my Spirit was trying to leave my body as I experienced the shock of this news. It was a bit like a car accident in which everything goes in slow motion and you're not really sure what is happening. While I was trying to get back in my body, he rambled on.

The doctor told me I had a small but aggressive cancer. He described it as curable. But my trust in him was not particularly high given my recent experience. He looked me in the eye as he spoke, but I couldn't help but feel betrayed since he had said it was nothing just a couple of days ago.

Over the next several days, I was whisked to multiple appointments. First an MRI of both breasts, then to a surgeon, then to a radiation oncologist, and then, finally, to an oncologist. The process felt mechanical, like I was on a conveyor belt.

In the appointment with the radiation oncologist, he explained that I would undergo seven weeks of whole breast radiation. When I heard the word "radiation," I literally felt my energy and Spirit take a step back. He went on to explain that the radiation would almost certainly ruin my implants, which I had loved since getting them years before, because of the scar tissue that would develop. Not to mention that the radiation would be right over my heart. When I asked if there were other alternatives, he said that in my case there were not.

Then my husband and I saw the surgeon, who spent all of fifteen minutes with us. After a brief physical examination, she explained—from the farthest side of the room and in the most generic language—that she would go in and take out the cancer, and then I'd be on my way. She asked if I had any questions. I said no. You don't know what you don't know, and I didn't have a freaking clue.

I booked the surgery for four weeks later, on the day after I was planning to deliver a talk to fifty people about *how our thoughts create our reality*. This was my first big public-speaking engagement, and it was part of my second-year thesis for my master's degree. It was important to me, and I wanted to have all of my faculties. My husband and the surgeon wanted the surgery to happen right away, and I was calm and centered, knowing that I needed to deliver this talk with clarity. I also couldn't help but notice the brilliant, albeit terrifying, opportunity the Universe had presented to me: I would be able to "walk my talk" during my presentation.

As the days passed, I educated myself on my options, and based on what I was facing, I was seriously leaning toward a mastectomy, as a lumpectomy would also require seven weeks of whole breast radiation, which would damage and put scar tissue on my breast implants. I didn't want a deformed breast. I was a young, beautiful girl. I wanted to wear a bikini! I also knew that I didn't want to subject any of my bodies—mental, physical, emotional, or spiritual—to heavy dosages of radiation every day for seven weeks.

I found myself in circles where people were talking about *second opinions* on several occasions. It hadn't even occurred to me to get a second opinion, as the team of doctors I had met with seemed competent and sure of themselves and the treatment options seemed straightforward. Yet, after the third "second opinion" conversation I found myself in, it was crystal clear to me that the Universe was trying to get my attention. (As a side note, I *always* pay close attention to anything that comes into my awareness in threes. I see this as a direct "hello" from the Universe, and if I ignore whatever it is, I'll probably miss out on something.)

I called my plastic surgeon, whom I love. (When he had done my augmentation years ago, the last thing he had said to me before I went under anesthesia was, "Your worst fear is either that you'll wake up and they'll be too big or that you'll wake up and they'll be too small?" I awoke to perfect breasts.) He referred me to another surgeon at a different hospital.

Off I went, headed to "a date" with a new doctor. My husband and I knew right away that something was different, as this doctor's office gave me a nice cotton spa robe to wear as opposed to a paper-towel wraparound, which was what the other office had given me. Dr. Lisa Guerra came in. She sat knee to knee with us and looked me in the eye. She spent more time connecting with me and my husband than the previous surgeon had during our entire meeting. TWO AND A HALF HOURS later, she had explained, in great detail, what breast cancer was, what type I had, every possible option for treatment, every rabbit hole, and every potential complication. She also told me about a new technology that was an alternative to whole breast radiation; it was called interoperative radiation therapy. She said that IORT took place on the table during the surgery, while under anesthesia, and that it lasted just eight minutes. If I was interested, I could see if I qualified for the new treatment. She then told me that the device with which they administered the IORT *was shaped like a fishhook!*

The emotions welled up inside of me. I knew immediately that this was my course of treatment and *decided internally* that I would "qualify" for this treatment, which I did. I felt energy running through my body, and I *knew* that this was the right path for me. My husband and I left her office, and both of us were astonished by the genuine care, compassion, and incredible medical service we had just witnessed. I cried, grateful that I had followed my intuition.

My husband said, "That other appointment was almost criminal."

I looked at him, tears streaming down my face, and retorted, "Fifteen-minute consultation?" At the time, we had really thought that was okay.

We went to lunch, and I knew deep inside that everything was going to be okay.

From that point forward, navigating my breast cancer became the most important thing in my life. I have a type-A, driver personality and have spent much of my life pushing myself everywhere I wanted to go. With my breast cancer diagnosis, I had to stop and *be* with myself in a way that was new to me. I had never before given myself that level of true compassion and genuine nurturing. I attribute this, of course, to my education at USM. Because of the gentle compassion with which I treated myself, my road to being cancer-free unfolded with ease and grace. Looking back on it all, it was really quite miraculous.

While this new illness in my life wasn't a secret, it also wasn't something I was talking about in the way the "old me" would have. The "old me" would've been seeking sympathy for what was happening to me. However, I delivered my talk in front of fifty people and never once mentioned my diagnosis.

Before my surgery, I came to understand my inner truth. I knew the cause of this major imbalance, and in my heart and Soul, I knew the cure. All of the recent changes I had made—quitting my job, starting my own consultancy, meditating daily, walking, juicing, and pursuing my personal spiritual path—were *intuitive steps* that were one step ahead of this cancer. The cancer was the last concentrated residual that needed to free itself from my body. The cancer was leftover garbage that needed to be removed. The cancer was the acknowledgment of what had its hook in me and my ability to transcend it.

Two years earlier, I had experienced my frozen shoulder. That physical issue interrupted my life in every way possible, and I was pissed off about it. It was annoying, it was costing me time and money, and it was forcing me to slow down. At that time, my frozen shoulder was *happening to me*. I had not yet made the shift to seeing life as *happening for me*. It was the relentless pain in my shoulder that prompted me to practice meditation as a way to manage the pain. It was my shoulder that forced me to leave work on a medical leave of absence, and while I was away I came to recognize that my body, mind, and spirit were exhausted from the way I was living my life. It was the realization that I needed to have so that I could start making some serious changes to the way I was living. And while the cancer was very attention-getting, the shoulder pain was what first got me to make some changes. The cancer diagnosis was the SUPER-CLEAR invitation from the Universe to actually live life differently, not just to talk or think about it differently.

Let's explore Higher Guidance at a deeper level, looking at how your intuition operates and where it comes from, so you can begin to listen more deeply to your Higher Guidance, which will allow you to take Spirit-guided actions that create a richer, more meaningful, and more fulfilled life.

Discerning Between the Ego and Higher Guidance

As an energetic body that has an infinite aspect, Higher Guidance is always available to you. This Higher Guidance is actually coming directly from that higher, infinite part of you. It's coming from your Higher Self. Your Authentic Self. Whatever you want to call it. It's coming from your Soul, the part of you that is connected to All That Is.

The brilliance of the intuition coming from your Higher Self is that it has a higher perspective than your learned, small self does. You are in your physical body on the ground (Planet Earth), and your ego has a narrow view of your life. Your Soul, because it's higher and because it resides outside of physical time and space, can see further. It has information that your ego is not privy to from its limited vantage point.

Imagine the difference between standing at the bottom of a mountain and standing at the top of it. From the top, you can see much farther. You can identify obstacles that are in the way or see a pot of gold farther down the path. The lower perspective is in the valley and cannot see these things. At the bottom, you think that the logical path to a goal is one particular way, and from the mountaintop, your Soul can see that if you take that path, you will fall into a canyon. However, if you follow a path that doesn't make logical sense, it is actually the quickest and most rewarding path, as you'll avoid having to climb out of a canyon that you can't even see from your point of view.

How do you tell the difference between information that is coming to you from your higher internal-guidance system— from your Soul—and information that is coming to you from your ego? Information from your internal-guidance system (our intuition) is calm and clear yet subtle and gentle. This information can wait because it's always available to you. It's just a matter of whether you are willing to pay attention to it or not. This information comes from a loving place and gives you a sense of knowing. This information gives you a feeling of inner authenticity. The energy of this information is peaceful, loving, and trusting.

Tuning into energy you feel is a strategic way to sort through the information and determine if it is coming from your intuition or your ego. When you are receiving guidance from your intuition, there is a sense of calm. I know, it would be nice if your intuition was louder. And listening to your intuition is a choice. If your intuition were YELLING at you, you wouldn't have the choice to listen; you would *have* to listen. One reason why you don't hear and follow your intuition is because when you're going up against the loud demands of your ego, sometimes your intuition gets trampled. This is why getting quiet and feeling the energy is so helpful.

In her wonderful audiobook *Advanced Energy Anatomy*, Caroline Myss shares, "First thought, best thought." When I heard this, it was the permission I needed so that I could listen to my intuition and stop questioning myself, constantly thinking about and reviewing all of the "logical" things in my head.

To me, intuitive information provides a sense of "knowing," a sense of being on the right path. This information *feels* peaceful and trustworthy inside of you. Being able to really tune into the feeling that is connected to the thought is extremely helpful. Information you receive from your Higher Self is always underscored with peacefulness and calmness. It's the illogical, nonsensical aspect of the information itself that can sometimes encourage your ego to create fear around whatever your intuition brings forward.

Information from the Ego

Information that is coming from your learned self—your personality or your ego—is urgent and demanding and insists on being right. The ego can be relentless and repetitive. It is often loud and can feel forceful. The ego is caught up in judgment. This is a major clue right here: If there is right and wrong associated with the information you are receiving; you can know it's coming from the ego.

The ego often tramples over your intuition. This is self-sabotage. This underscores the importance of being quiet. Remember, the ego will fight for safety, security, comfort, and control. If the information you are receiving threatens any of these areas, the ego will send up the fear flag. (When I heard, "Quit your six-figure job without a plan," my ego pushed back!)

The ego wants life to be logical. It wants everything to look perfect and pretty and organized. The ego can only base future decisions on the collected data from the past, and it will measure the past and think it knows what will happen in the future. This is often what makes you sabotage the inspiration you receive from the infinite part of your being. Your ego is comprised of a series of learned behaviors and experiences. Again, I want to stress that it's almost like a computer database. And when you are seeking to do something new in your life, your ego wants to check the "database" for any information it has collected that can inform the choices you make going forward. And since you've never actually done that thing you are inspired by before, the database may not actually have any information to reference, which can easily cause your ego to shut down the whole idea.

Again, tune into the feeling around the thought. Connect to your heart instead of your head and *feel* the information you are receiving. If you feel calm and peaceful, it's your intuition; if you feel a sense of urgency and fear, it's your ego.

Your Body Is a Highly Attuned Transmitter

Your body receives the information from your Higher Self. This is what makes it intuition. Whether or not you want to follow the guidance you're receiving is up to you. The way you feel when you receive the information can help you identify whether your Higher Self or your ego is sending the information.

I ignored my deeper, intuitive truth, and my outer body reflected my inner pain. I knew I was unhappy in my career, yet I didn't do anything about it. I remained stuck because I had no evidence in my "computer database" that supported the idea that I could do anything different than what I had been doing for the previous twenty-eight years of my life. My learned self kept telling me that I had to work hard and suffer to make a good living, that I didn't have the time to rebuild a new career, and that I wouldn't be able to get a salary that would support the life I had built during my long tenure. So, I remained frozen, continuing to live with those limiting beliefs. Thus, my inner problems turned into an outer problem: adhesive capsulitis. A FROZEN shoulder.

Paying attention to what feelings are connected to the thoughts you have can guide you out of the place you are in. Feelings that are in accordance with your Authentic Self and the information you receive from your Higher Self are indicative of your true nature. According to science, those feelings have a higher vibratory frequency to them and give the physical feeling of lightness. These are feelings such as peace, calm, centeredness, joy, inner knowing, expansiveness, and freedom.

Feelings with a lower vibratory frequency invoke feelings of heaviness and contraction, such as anxiety, insecurity, tension, and urgency. Because your true nature is comprised of the energy of Love, you can conclude that the negative, low frequency emotions, which are *driven by fear*, are always coming from the ego or the learned self.

Intuition Is Often Illogical

The single biggest reason people don't listen to and trust their intuition is because much of the time, the big things seem totally and completely illogical and irrational. Your reasonable mind distracts you from really engaging with your intuition, because it's nonsensible. However, you must remember that your Soul has a higher perspective. Your Soul is actually giving you the most direct route to get where you are going. It just may not make sense to your logical mind.

Intuition can also go against your status quo. It has the potential to rock the boat, to upset the apple cart, and to invite you to make changes that may disrupt your life and the lives of those around you. Mostly, I have found, in my own experience, that in most instances I initially didn't have the courage to act on my intuition. In truth, it wasn't that I didn't hear it. I heard it. We always hear it. I just chose to ignore it, to not make eye contact with it, and to instead allow my ego's fear to run the show. I know now that learning to be strong and courageous and learning to follow my intuition are some of the lessons in my Soul's plan.

Everyone is intuitive. This is not something that is a special gift for only some people. Everyone has it. EVERYONE! It's just a matter of trusting the messages you are hearing and being courageous enough to act on them. Trusting and acting on your intuition will absolutely improve your relationship with it. And again, to be clear, everyone is intuitive and is regularly receiving Higher Guidance. Yes, even you.

When You Can't Decide

Based on my experience, I can tell you that you are being invited to follow your Higher Guidance when you can't decide something. I heard a repeated whisper from deep within my Soul that was telling me I should quit my job and my multiple-decade career in hospitality. I was miserable and was having health challenges, and the longer I remained where I was, the more miserable and sicker I became. Yet, because my tenure in hospitality allowed me to have my ego's perception of safety, security, comfort, and control, my logical mind wouldn't allow me to quit. This literally went on for *years*.

Let me also add in a side note about "comfort." In truth, I wasn't *really* comfortable; it was an illusion. I was physically ill, I was suffering from mental and emotional anguish, and I was spiritually bankrupt at the time. Nothing about this was *really* comfortable, but it sure was *familiar*. It was known to me. And in that familiarity, in that "comfort" zone, I had the illusion of safety.

As you know, I did quit, and I did reinvent my life. I knew from the first whisper that leaving that career and reinventing myself was the *most fulfilling* path for me, but because I didn't listen for such a long time, I experienced a great deal more of suffering.

In your own life, what are some occasions when you had conflicting information? When you decided to do something and then someone said something "bad" about it, did you second-guess yourself? When an idea came to you but then your logical mind got front and center and talked you right out of it, did you find yourself in a perpetual quandary?

I have learned that when you ignore the golden rule of "first thought, best thought," as taught by Caroline Myss, you are often going against your Higher Guidance. One of my clients continued to ignore her intuition, which was telling her that her boyfriend was being dishonest. She went through a great deal of emotional suffering, and it eventually escalated into a horrific event in which the truth was revealed. She looks back on this now and can honestly say, "Deep down, I knew. It just seemed illogical, and I didn't want to believe it."

The Way I Thought It Was *Supposed* to Be

Had I not made those changes, who knows where I'd be. The way I thought I was *supposed* to live life was a *big* misunderstanding. I had the limiting belief that I should work sixty hours a week and ignore the calling of my heart. I had the limiting belief that feeling exhausted and in pain was normal.

Ignoring the pleading voice inside, which I had tried to silence for so many years, was a recipe for disease. When I was caught up in these sixty-hour weeks, I had to use my free time to repair and provide basic maintenance to my body. I was visiting a chiropractor, an energy healer, and a massage therapist, and that's not to mention the beauty schedule, which included hair, nails, and eyebrows. All of this was part of my weekend agenda, and on Monday I would just wake up and do it all again. Work, work, work. Bouts of insomnia. Up at 2:00 a.m. Thinking about work. Showering while thinking about work. Skipping breakfast to get to work sooner. Splintering my energies into a million pieces before I ever even got to work. Eating a lousy lunch so I could get back to work. Getting home late, and my whole Being consumed with stress and anxiety. Ignoring my Spirit. Repeat. Week after week, month after month, for twenty-eight consecutive years.

Had I not stopped that pattern, the cancer would still be there. It would still be aggressively growing. It would've grown silently, and it would've gone undetected because I would not have noticed the lump nor had a dream about it. And even if I had dreamed about it, because of my busy, left-brained chatter, I would have been highly unlikely to have remembered the dream. And by the time I discovered the lump, it would have been too late. I probably would have been dead by now.

But that's not what happened. Today, I am alive and cancer-free. Today, I am thriving in my life. I am connected, and I am guided. I am seeing beauty and perfection in my life, and this is happening because I'm slowing down, listening to my intuition, and being courageous enough to act on it. My life bloomed when I finally began listening to that little voice that had been trying to get my attention for so long. It has opened my heart to my Spirit, to the Universe, and to everything and everyone around me. It has invited me to be vulnerable as well as grateful for all of my experiences. It has shifted my perspective, and now I know that *all* of our experiences—no matter how traumatizing, difficult, or ugly they may appear—are invited by our Souls and are orchestrated with divine perfection *for our own growth and learning* in this life. I have also come to know that I am not smarter than the Universe. My life is happening for *my highest good*, even if it doesn't feel like it at times. I had to learn to give up control and trust myself to realize that. I had to transcend my hook, my ego.

Ever since that "second opinion" day, I have deeply honored and revered my Higher Guidance. That was the day I decided I was no longer going to ignore that inner voice or negotiate with my logic, regardless of how irrational my intuition sometimes seemed to be.

I've heard Caroline Myss say that most of us don't have the courage to listen to our intuition. Yet when we do listen and respond to its illogical, irrational tugs, it becomes a natural self-esteem builder and a natural elixir that strengthens our self-worth. From personal experience, I can say that this is entirely true. When you listen to your intuition, it removes your need to seek answers outside of yourself. When you can simply tune in and *hear* the guidance that is always being given, then have the courage to take action, you begin to build the muscle of trust with yourself, your life, and God.

Now that you have more clarity on how to tell the difference between the voice of your Higher Guidance and the voice of your learned, small self, let's do a review. You are a unique, individualized expression of a magnificent, divine energy that is everywhere. This is the same energy that comprises All That Is. You are part of that. Your Soul chose to incarnate and have a physical experience. The purpose of your existence in this third-dimensional realm is to remember who you truly are: an expression of the energy of Love. This expression unfolds over a lifetime as you discover and create your path, experiencing the love that you seek. This journey can be clouded with self-defeating thoughts and old, convoluted belief systems. The unraveling of these misunderstandings and old belief systems reveals your Soul's plan for your human growth and evolution.

Take a breath. Now, you can begin take a greater level of responsibility for the game you are playing, or you can run and hide. You can begin to believe that you are a divine creator, or you can keep pretending. You already know, and choice is yours.

In the next chapter, I will shine the light on a tool that is the bridge between your Higher Self and your Human Self.

Opportunity for Transformation
Take Action

This is the seventh Opportunity for Transformation. This is your chance to take action and move your life forward, discover a new part of your consciousness, and create an experience for yourself that will deepen your learning of this material. All of the OFTs are designed to assist you in more fully integrating Original Wisdom from your Authentic Self into your day-to-day life. If you would like to download an actual worksheet or listen to an audio version of this OFT, please visit donnabond.com/opportunityfortransformation.

Higher Guidance Exercise

Reflect on a time when you *did* use your intuition and it led you to something greater. Maybe it led you to a more expanded version of yourself or to a memorable experience or connection in your life. What happened? What was the experience of receiving the guidance like? Was it subtle? Did you have to negotiate with your ego? Write about these examples in your journal. Pay attention to how you feel in your body with each consideration.

Identify a situation in your life right now where you are receiving conflicting information from your Higher Guidance (your Soul's calling) and your ego (logical mind).

Reflect on something that you feel inspired by, though other "outside people and influences" are giving you different advice and guidance, squelching your feelings of aliveness.

As you explore all of these situations involving your intuition and the Higher Guidance that is available to you, will you make a different choice? Are you ready to listen more?

Sacred Truth Activation

This is the seventh Sacred Truth Activation. Find a quiet, private space to center yourself, light a candle, and speak these words aloud. If you would like to listen to an audio version of this guided personal decree, please visit donnabond.com/sacredtruthactivations.

I Am Accessing Higher Guidance

I am naturally intuitive, and I am easily accessing Higher Guidance. I am open to receiving Higher Guidance from my Soul. I am open to allowing my ego, or my learned self, to be in service to my Soul. I am aware I easily hear, see, sense, and feel the guidance because there is a communication link between me and my Higher Self. I am open and available to this wisdom, and I allow it to flow into my learned self. I know that I am so loved and guided by my Essential Nature, my Soul. I am aware that the information that comes through can feel nonsensical to my logical mind. I am aware that my inner knowing and Higher Guidance come gently and calmly into my consciousness. I am also aware that only I can act on the information that I am receiving. As I take action that is in accordance with the guidance I receive, I build trust and confidence in myself. I am trusting that relying on my intuition is safe. I am also aware that when my outer circumstances seem disorganized, this is what it looks like when the Universe is working things out for my highest good. I am easily and calmly dwelling in a place of trust inside myself as I continue to be fully open to the guidance being given to me by my Soul.

I acknowledge and affirm that I am easily receiving guidance in a way that works for me. I am aware that when I have thoughts that seem urgent or demanding or that are driven by fear, these thoughts are coming from my ego, or small self. I am aware that guidance is always available, and I see that this guidance is beautifully directing my life. I am becoming more courageous, and I am acting on the intuitive guidance I am receiving. I am aware that guidance from my Higher Self feels peaceful, centered, joyful, and firmly grounded in a place of love and knowing. I am aware this guidance feels lighter and expansive, though my small self may perceive it as illogical.

To get to the top of the Tor, one must climb the seven terraces. This spiritual number is representative of the seven levels of consciousness, which include waking consciousness, deep sleep, dreaming, transcendental consciousness, cosmic consciousness, God consciousness, and unity consciousness. The seven tiers wrapping around the Tor make up a three-dimensional labyrinth. Entering such a labyrinth takes one into the abyss of the unknown. The goddess must transcend the unknown to reach her fullest expression, which indeed activates the full integration of all of the multidimensional aspects of her sweet self.

To successfully travel the path of the uncharted, undiscovered, unfamiliar, and unknown, it is necessary to light the way. It is fundamental to let go of total reliance on one's Human Self and to begin trusting in one's Higher Self, and Higher Power. The process begins with the goddess accepting responsibility for this inherent power that exists within her. This reclamation of her innate Source bursts out of her in an exclamation of profound knowing: "I am that!"

Chapter Eight

The Responsibility of "I AM"

"The words *I am,* which you consistently use to define who
you are and what you are capable of, are holy expressions
for the name of God—the highest aspect of yourself."

~ Wayne Dyer

I learned through the teachings of American self-help author
and motivational speaker Wayne Dyer, St. Germain, and other
wisdom teachers that anything you think or say after the words
"I AM" initiate God into action. Because stating "I AM" is in
alignment with the higher part of yourself and your Soul, what
you proclaim to the world with the language of an "I AM" statement is your power. It is an activation of that energetic part of
you that is a creator. "I AM" is a magic formula that can be used
to create, expand, and design your life. Practice it as you would a
magic spell in order to call into being whatever you connect to it.

Pay particular attention to the limiting, sometimes less aware,
self-defeating, self-sabotaging, negative ways you might be
using "I AM." (Remember those limiting beliefs from chapter
six?) "I AM" is a magic power that you hold, so infuse your

power with Original Wisdom. Practice affirming statements in which you make a conscious investment with your energetic power. *I am happy. I am joyful. I am vibrant, flexible, and alive. I am co-creating the divine design of my life.*

How the Power of "I AM" Shaped My Experience

Taking responsibility for my health was up to me, and the empowering discovery of "I AM" gave me an epiphany. Suddenly, it was clear how I had invested energy in a *miscreation*. My frozen shoulder was a perfect example of how I continued to perpetuate pain and suffering in my life; I invested my energy (Higher Self) in and put my physical attention on what I did *not* want. I went around and told *everyone* who would listen what was wrong with me: "I am suffering from a frozen shoulder. I am only able to lift my arm this high. I am in constant pain. I am exhausted. I feel like crap. I am too tired to do anything but complain about this pain." Blah, blah, blah. Even I got tired of listening to myself.

My dear friend and coach Johnna once said to me, "When are *you* going to take responsibility for your health and the way you feel?"

I was taken aback. I said, "Uh…what do you mean? I'm doing everything I can to fix the problem. I'm seeing physical therapists and acupuncturists and energy healers. I'm getting massages, exercising, and seeing my doctors."

She said gently, "Yes, but when are *you* going to de-cide (she always emphasized the "de" when she said decide) that *you* are in charge of your overall health and well-being?"

She explained lovingly that all of the things I was "doing" were outside of me and that the story I was telling was the energetic blueprint for the experience I was having. She helped me connect the dots, and that suddenly made it crystal clear. The vision I was creating needed to begin with *a belief that flowed from me.*

I was struck on a deep level with the understanding that in order to change the experience I was having with my health, I needed to mentally and emotionally embody a particular "way of being," And this way of being could only come from inside of me, not outside of me, which was where I had been perpetually seeking answers regarding my health. This way of being wasn't something I could *do.*

As I began to take a greater level of ownership and responsibility for what I wanted to create, I became aware that my language and use of the term "I AM" helped me change the core beliefs that actually perpetuated the experience of having a frozen shoulder. I saw immediately how I had continued to exacerbate the issue with the powerful word choices and energy I was misusing. When the power of "I AM" came into my awareness, my consciousness began paying close attention to the words coming out of my mouth and, more importantly, to the thoughts that were repeating in my head.

I left Johnna and went home to create an "Ideal Scene" regarding my health. (Making an Ideal Scene is a tool you can use to make conscious intentions a "way of life." We learned this at USM.) The focal point was the health I *desired.* Although I was still very much in pain and did not feel vibrant and healthy at the time, I began reciting daily affirmations about my overall health and well-being, and they all began with those two magic words: I AM. I began to embody a way of being in my Ideal Scene, and it went like this: "I am aliveness. I am flexible. I am feeling amazing. I am waking up refreshed and rejuvenated. I am feeling an endless supply of energy. I am whole and healthy." I began to say these words out loud every day, even when I felt like dog poop. I began to *be, to embody,* the vibrational match to the healthy state I desired. I began to *come from* the place of radiant health in my life experience rather than trying to get "to" it. I did my best to embody the idea of it, to imagine what it looked and felt like, and from that place of believing it was possible, my health magically began to transform. When I made the inner shift and began speaking the experience I wanted to have into existence, believing it was possible, my physical health truly began to improve. My shoulder really began to heal.

I once worked with a client who had terrible arthritis. Her whole world was about arthritis and pain. She wanted to help people learn how to manage and move past their pain in the incredible way that she was able to. She wanted to teach healing by sharing her own experience of healing. As we spoke, I couldn't help but reflect to her that everything she was saying was positioning the pain of arthritis at the center of her world. She thought about it, she spoke about it, and she told stories about it. Pain was literally the center of her Universe. I invited her to consider stepping *out* of the pain of arthritis and *into* the idea of optimal health, flexibility, and movement with ease and grace. Instead of even saying phrases such as, "I am pain-free," I suggested she completely eliminate her focus on pain altogether and begin to use words and ideas revolving around vitality, ease, comfort, mobility, and flexibility. This simple awareness invited a huge epiphany for her. She became aware it was her responsibility to shift her focus and her storytelling.

Energy flows where our attention goes. Sometimes we are unknowingly perpetuating the pain and suffering by simply keeping it in such a close proximity and view.

Calling Forward the Creator You Are

"I AM" is the presence of the Being within. "I AM" can be used for creation by connecting your words and thoughts to the experience you desire to have. "I AM" is essentially the name of the energy within you, and when you use these sacred words, you are taking responsibility for your life. You're enlisting the help of the higher part of yourself—the energetic, multidimensional part of you. "I AM" is your powerful connection to Source, and by acknowledging it you're recognizing that "I AM connected to All That Is."

Using the language of "I AM" is a way for you to stand in your authentic power, fulfill the Law of Magnetic Attraction, and bring into your experience that which you are affirming. "I AM" ignites the vibration of what you want to draw into your life. "I AM" is charged with power because it's a statement in the present tense about the present moment, and it calls forward the energy of your multidimensional self. No one can say "I AM" on your behalf. Only you can use these two little words and access the energetic power that they assemble. When you accept you are the creator of *your* life, "I AM" is a pivotal tool for transformation.

The Old Programs Connected to Your "I AM"

Often, the patterns that are repeating in your mind and your life are directly connected to your limiting beliefs. "I am tired. I am too busy. I am sick. I am not enough." They have been playing in your head for so long, beneath the surface, that they have put tracks down in your mind. I think of it as train tracks. When you have a negative thought, that thought just easily runs along this track because it has been laid down with such strength for so long.

Once you have an awareness of the power of "I AM," you can then begin to consciously reprogram your patterns. The first step in this is "catching" the negative train as it's zooming down the track. When you can see it happening—when you can become the observer and be aware of your own thoughts—you can then interrupt the pattern and "envision" the new track you want to lay down.

When you speak or think, your word choice sends a message to you and communicates to the Universe. What are you attracting into your life when you misuse the power of "I AM"? For example, "I am tired. I am busy. I am sick." You can reprogram your thoughts, your experiences, and your life when you can make the shift into saying, "I am radiant. I am vitality. I am aliveness. I am joy. I am love. I am abundant."

"I AM" as a Tool for Transformation

Using "I AM" in a statement of affirmation, assertion, pronouncement, or declaration is a way to get you from here to there. Using "I AM" as a declaration of what you want to create, or of where you want to be, allows you to become the match to it energetically, thus bringing it squarely into your experience that much sooner.

Where you can get tripped up is in overcoming the mentality of "I AM NOT." Universal Energy doesn't recognize these types of negative statements. For example, it's less supportive to say, "I am not overweight," or to say, "I am not broke," because the Universe will focus in on the words "overweight" and "broke." Why? Because that is what you are focusing on. By using" I AM NOT," you're just attracting more of what you don't want. Instead, you want to flip those statements into positives, saying, "I am my ideal, healthy weight," or saying, "I am abundant." While you are first trying on your new affirmations, they may feel cumbersome and untrue. I find it helpful to *identify real evidence* that supports the belief you are moving into.

If you will recall, we did this before, using the example of feeling supported. The limiting belief was, "I have to do everything myself," and we tried to replace this with a new belief. We started with this realization: "The chair that I'm sitting on is supporting me." Therefore, our theoretical person had real-world evidence that he or she was being supported.

Let's look at this simple phrase: "I am abundant." You can go on a fact-finding mission to find all of the ways this idea is true. This is what supports you in being the vibrational match in your consciousness. Here is the evidence: "I am aware of the abundance of sky above me. I am feeling an abundance of air flowing into my lungs. I am seeing an abundance of thread on the carpet. I am recognizing the abundant and tireless beats of my heart." You get the idea. The exercise corrals your thoughts in the direction you want them to go in.

It's also important to use the present tense instead of the future tense when it comes to the Law of Attraction. When you say, "One day, I will be…" this phrasing keeps whatever it is away from you. "I will be" also means "I am not now." You have to learn to overcome the urge to use the future tense when you are creating affirmations and using the power of "I AM." State your intention in the NOW, as if it's already happening. This is a key element in this transformational practice. By stating the affirmation in the "now," you access the energetic power of the present moment. This is the point of creation. It's not in the future, and you know it's not in the past. Everything you want to create happens in the *now*.

Although it's easy to get hung up in the physical world and allow your logical mind to believe only what you can see, you can begin to shape your experience by beginning with "I AM" statements about the experience you want to have. Even though you may not be having the experience yet, you can clearly define what it looks like, and through the magic formula of "I AM," you will quickly see how it begins to align with your experience, as that becomes the story you are telling yourself and the Universe. You will update your belief system with your new "I AM" statements.

In physical reality, you are taught to pursue, to achieve, to chase, and to set goals. You are taught to always pursue something, and then you buy into the lie that the achievement (or arrival to)—whatever it is—will give you the happiness and fulfillment you seek. It actually doesn't work this way. Largely, in part, because this is pursuing something outside of yourself. Once you *become* what you desire to attain or have, you then are the match to that, and the Universe can't help but give you what you desire.

I know it might seem totally counterintuitive, especially considering everything you were taught. In the context of all that you've learned thus far, though, this is exactly why you can begin to trust it. Or at least strongly consider. I invite you to test it out for yourself.

You can also be mindful of the fact that the most important person you are sharing this with is yourself. You are the most important person in your life experience. "I AM" is a self-empowering, self-honoring practice to reshape core beliefs. It is how *you* define *you* in the physical world. It's how you call forward your Life Force energy and how you use the power of creation inside of you.

Your life is the reflection of whatever you connect to with your "I AM."

Your "I AM" Is the True You

This is your opportunity to call forward the creator you are and begin to play a more participatory role in creating a life that you love and that you want to experience. It's about accepting that some of the beliefs you have been taught up until now have diminished the true, authentic power you have inside of you as a divine, spiritual Being having a human adventure.

As an energy system that is connected to All That Is, you're using the power of thought and belief to shape the experience you desire to have in this life. Revealing the unique, individualized expression of yourself *is* your purpose in this life. To do this, you're required to strip away anything that is untrue.

You are being guided. This wisdom-filled Higher Self, or Soul essence, inside of you is leading the way. This is the part of you that holds the keys to the kingdom. It has the map. It knows the plan. It is the embodiment of your Original Wisdom. Developing a relationship with this part of your Being means you are bridging the gap between your learned ego/personality and the part of you that is connected to All That Is. In acknowledging this relationship, you will experience greater levels of success in your life. Recognizing the love that you are is a revelation. Allowing your humanness to experience your spiritual nature is how you can fill the void inside of yourself and start to feel whole. Nothing in the outside world can make you whole. Nothing you can buy or consume or do will make you whole. Not even anyone you date or marry will make you feel whole. The only way to feel whole is through the integration of your divine, spiritual nature.

As you begin to allow your Higher Self to guide your life, you will most certainly be invited to stretch yourself. Now that you have the tools that will guide you along the rest of the way, you are ready to leave the familiarity of your comfort zone in order to evolve into the next phase of your entelechy. Leaving the known and crossing the abyss into the unknown delivers many gifts. As you give yourself permission to envision your next level of potential, it's time for you to trust your Soul to guide you through it. Even when it feels uncomfortable. Listening to the often-illogical inspiration of your Higher Self is one thing; having the courage to take action based on the guidance you receive is another. Find support. Community is important. Remember, anytime you step out of your comfort zone, past the safe space of familiarity, *fear* materializes. This fact, I am afraid, is a built-in part of the human adventure. Yet, as you learn to transcend your fear, you can even become comfortable with being uncomfortable.

In the next chapter, I'll invite you to claim the greatest gifts that you are given when you have the courage to transcend fear.

Opportunity for Transformation
Take Action

This is the eighth Opportunity for Transformation. This is your chance to take action and move your life forward, discover a new part of your consciousness, and create an experience for yourself that will deepen your learning of this material. All of the OFTs are designed to assist you in more fully integrating Original Wisdom from your Authentic Self into your day-to-day life. If you would like to download an actual worksheet or listen to an audio version of this OFT, please visit donnabond.com/opportunityfortransformation.

"I AM" Reflection Exercise

Take one area of your life where you are experiencing some discontent and create an "I AM Reflection" of the experience you desire. In this exercise, you are intentionally envisioning a new reality until it becomes your new reality.

First, invite in the guidance from your Higher Self, your Authentic Self. Allow this part of you to guide the vision. Create your "I AM Reflection" by looking through the lens of Love with enthusiasm and gratitude. Create from a place of Original Wisdom and authentic empowerment. You'll do this by stating your vision statements in the first person and in the NOW. Write the statements in the present tense, as if they are already happening. Allow your Authentic Self to guide you as you create your new reflections by inviting in the high qualities of the Authentic Self. Some of these qualities are depicted on the graphic named "I Am Reflections" on page 160. They include

Neutrality, Oneness, Joy, Authenticity, Acceptance, Compassion, Unconditional Loving, and Reverence. These are qualities that naturally emanate from your Soul, or Higher Self, and you can invoke them by opening your heart and seeing your life through the lens of Love.

For the sake of your ego, it is important that your "I AM Reflections" feel believable. Part of the reason you're creating and affirming these statements is to shift your consciousness into the space of believing something more is possible for you. Creating statements that support all levels of your consciousness (spiritual, mental, emotional, and physical) is helpful in wholly supporting yourself.

For example, if you feel overwhelmed and out of time, you can set an intention that looks like this: "I am so joy-filled and grateful. I am filled with aliveness. I am filled with vitality. I am feeling energetic. I am so happy and am filled with gratitude. Now that I am filled with enthusiasm daily, I am in the flow of life. I am exactly where I am supposed to be. I am so happy and grateful now that I am present in my life and present with every person in every situation. I am so happy and grateful now that I am experiencing deep, authentic levels of joy, love, and aliveness."

Integrating Your Higher Self and Your Human Self

In the "SPIRITUAL" section of the worksheet below, notice how you can call forward the assistance of your "I AM" presence (Your Authentic Self) in order to activate and illuminate your intentions. Invoke this higher, wisdom-filled self and call forth the human qualities naturally embodied by your Authentic Self. Qualities such as Neutrality, Oneness, Joy, Authenticity,

Acceptance, Honesty, and Ease. Connecting through your heart, invoke Original Wisdom, Enthusiasm, Unconditional Loving, Peace, Aliveness, and Reverence. Infuse these beautiful qualities at the mental, emotional, and physical levels. Hold the intention to fully integrate all levels of your consciousness. Articulate your "I AM" intentions to reflect what you'd love to experience in regard to each of the sections on the worksheet.

Now, formulate statements that support your mental, emotional, and physical levels and allow your spiritual level of consciousness to help guide you through this process. As all of this comes together, you embody a new way of being, and this tool becomes a way for you to more wholly participate in activating your intentions.

In the MENTAL section, you will develop "I AM" statements about the *thoughts* you place your attention on.

In the EMOTIONAL section, you will formulate statements that support the *feelings* you want to experience.

In the PHYSICAL section, you will articulate the actions and *behaviors* that will support you in co-creating your intentions. For example: If you feel exhausted, overwhelmed, and out of time, you might create something that looks like the "I Am Reflection" illustration.

Once you create your "I AM Reflection," use the completed worksheet as a tool. Place your focus and attention on it frequently, and it will act as a guidepost that assists and supports you in bringing your new reality into view. If you'd like to download a blank copy of the "I AM Reflection" form, visit donnabond.com/Opportunityfortransformation.

I Am Reflections

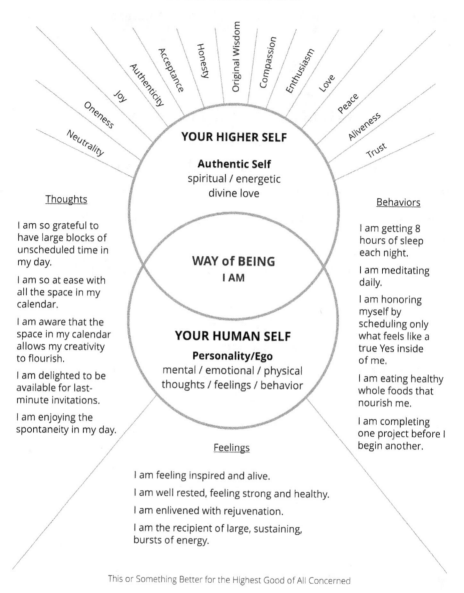

YOUR HIGHER SELF

Authentic Self
spiritual / energetic
divine love

WAY of BEING

I AM

YOUR HUMAN SELF

Personality/Ego
mental / emotional / physical
thoughts / feelings / behavior

Labels around arc: Neutrality · Oneness · Joy · Authenticity · Acceptance · Honesty · Original Wisdom · Compassion · Enthusiasm · Love · Peace · Aliveness · Trust

Thoughts

I am so grateful to have large blocks of unscheduled time in my day.

I am so at ease with all the space in my calendar.

I am aware that the space in my calendar allows my creativity to flourish.

I am delighted to be available for last-minute invitations.

I am enjoying the spontaneity in my day.

Behaviors

I am getting 8 hours of sleep each night.

I am meditating daily.

I am honoring myself by scheduling only what feels like a true Yes inside of me.

I am eating healthy whole foods that nourish me.

I am completing one project before I begin another.

Feelings

I am feeling inspired and alive.

I am well rested, feeling strong and healthy.

I am enlivened with rejuvenation.

I am the recipient of large, sustaining, bursts of energy.

This or Something Better for the Highest Good of All Concerned

Sacred Truth Activation

This is the eighth Sacred Truth Activation. Find a quiet, private space to center yourself, light a candle, and speak these words aloud. If you would like to listen to an audio version of this guided personal decree, please visit donnabond.com/sacredtruthactivations.

I AM

I am aware of the name of my Higher Self as the "I AM Presence." This is essentially my Spirit or my Soul. I am aware that as I say these words, I am creating a powerful vibrational alignment between what I state about myself and my life. I am aware that these two little words are only able to come from me and that when I am using these words, I am making a proclamation to the Universe. I am able to direct my experience and who I want to be by using this powerful pivot tool of transformation.

I am bringing my attention to the ways in which I misuse these two powerful words, in connection with where I place and how I direct my energy and attention. I am aware of how I have been using this magical and powerful affirmation in an unsupportive way up until now. I am taking full responsibility for how I choose to use these words, and I place my conscious attention on what I am connecting to with this powerful phrase. I am aware that the phrase "I AM" is a way I can merge with the larger, energetic Infinite Intelligence in the present moment. I am understanding now that only I can use the words "I AM." This brings a greater level of importance to what I attach to this phrase, as I am now more fully aware of my powers as a creator and how I am directing energy through my thoughts and with my attention.

I am aware that "I AM" is a formula I can use to create a life I want to experience. I am aware of how I am calling forward my Highest Self so that I can bring power to whatever I attach to the end of these sacred words. I am supporting myself in reshaping my thoughts. I am standing in my power as a creator as I use these words to design a life that is in alignment with what I want to experience.

As the goddess's clairvoyant sight has been awakened, she can now see the Otherworld. She has harnessed the power within. These new perceptions change her life forever. She now has full awareness of her divinity. Then comes the time when her activated powers must be fully trusted in her human form. Though she's confronted with doubt, she must now step directly through the unknown, meeting her darkest fears head-on, aware that true transformation can only take place on the actual back of the dragon. The alternative is to risk falling back asleep to the false lures of the "real" world.

Through the reclamation of her whole self, she aligns the resilience of her own humanness with the magnificence of her cosmic intelligence. The alchemical metamorphosis itself gifts her with the knowledge that she must *transform the dragon with Love, and in that she can harness its strength and make it her ally.*

Chapter Nine

The Alchemy of Fear

"As you learn to trust the unknown, life resolves
itself effortlessly and beautifully and a natural
process of deconditioning takes place inside you."

~ Richard Rudd

Control is such a pattern of conditioning—always knowing where you're going, planning out all the steps, figuring out the return on the investment, beginning with the end in mind. And while, of course, there is merit in visualizing your desired outcome—the state you want to experience—the learning is to leave enough space for the Universe to have its way with you.

As a recovering control freak, moving myself into a space in which I did not know the outcome in advance was scary for me. Being a marketing consultant and then a coach was perfect training for me. I had to face my fear and discover my resilience in the process. When you are self-employed, you no longer receive a regular paycheck. "Stepping off the cliff" and into the space of the unknown, where I had no idea where my next paycheck was coming from, was...well, TERRIFYING! I had to become totally reliant on the Self. Since then, I have made big strides in releasing control. I understand firsthand what this looks like and feels like in my body. I also know that as I continue to grow and expand, it requires me to repeatedly step out of my comfort zone.

The opportunity here is for you to begin to trust the Universe and to get comfortable with what Drs. Ron and Mary Hulnick call "the Divine Unknowing." The exciting thing about being in the Divine Unknowing is that you don't know what is going to happen. The totally freaking scary-as-shit thing about being in the Divine Unknowing is that you don't know what is going to happen. This can be exhilarating, actually, because you have just opened yourself up to unlimited possibilities. And, to your fragile ego—which craves safety, security, comfort, and control—it can be a place of fear and insecurity for the exact same reason.

This is where faith and trust become the only way to walk this path.

The Trust in Giving Up Control

When I first decided to quit my job and go out on my own as a marketing consultant, my plan was to have my former employer be my first client, as I would be able to train my successor. My former boss, however, refused to discuss the possibility of hiring me as a consultant until I resigned from my current position. He made it clear to me that I needed to resign *before* he would discuss hiring me as a marketing consultant.

What?! This was *not* the safety that I was hoping for. I wanted to be sure he would hire me *before* I quit. I wanted a "safety net" that was ready to catch me.

I had to accept that I had a 50/50 chance of having my former company become my first client. I had no other gigs lined up at the time, and things were unfolding so quickly that I was really taking a financial risk with this decision. To be honest, I was a little bit scared. Was this stupid?

I knew I had to change my situation because the internal discontent was so bad, and my physical health was in jeopardy. Even though there was no guarantee they would hire me, I was willing to take the risk. So, I did resign and then provided him with a proposal for the work I intended to do as their consultant. He waited to get back to me, saying that the resort owners needed to decide. I waited several weeks for a response.

During that waiting period, I danced back and forth with my fear. It would have been easy to have allowed my imagination to get carried away. *They won't hire me. I'll never be able to find another client. We will blow through our savings. I'll start fighting with my husband about money. We'll lose the house because we can't pay the mortgage.* WAIT! I was *not* going there! I refused to invest my energy in these ideas even though it was hard not to.

So, how did I occupy the chatter of my busy mind? I focused on managing my limiting thoughts around my financial security. I returned to my center, and remaining calm while living in the Divine Unknowing.. I put my energy—my Life Force— toward the idea that the Universe had my back. I told myself that because I was listening to my inner voice and taking action based on my inner truth, which was telling me to leave that job, I had to *trust* in whatever was about to happen next. Even though I didn't know what that was.

Finally, my boss invited me into his office. He sat me down with Shannon, who would be my successor. He said that they didn't want to hire me and that my newly formed company, Donna Bond Marketing, was not needed in order to support the transition.

I have complete recollection of what occurred inside of me in that moment. My heart did not skip a beat. My stomach did not do a flip-flop. I wasn't shocked. I was totally calm and still. Inside, I was residing in a place of absolute peace. In those seconds, a magical transformation took place. I had such reverence for myself, for my choice, and for my courage to take these steps. I had a deep level of trust within me that everything was happening as it should, and I really, *really* believed that in the core of my Being. In those fleeting moments, I had transcended my fear and found courage. I knew I would be okay somehow. In fact, I knew I would be better than okay.

A minute later, after he couldn't stand my silence any longer, my boss joyfully blurted out, "Just kidding! We want to hire you! Let's get your contract signed!" as he beamed at me with pride and admiration. My former boss likes to play big. The truth is that he has a big heart, and in that moment his heart was likely feeling tender, as we both realized we'd miss each other and the lively collaborations we had shared over the years.

I just shook my head at him, silently and secretly feeling so grateful to him for giving me the gift of that "temporary no." Now I had seen how I would respond when trusting myself and trusting the Universe. That day, my self-confidence, self-worth, and self-esteem grew in ways I never could have imagined. Not because I got hired, but because I thought I didn't.

Fear Itself Keeps Us Stuck

Oh, dear, sweet fear, wouldn't it be grand if we could make you go away? Wouldn't it be lovely if there were a magic pill we could take that would dissolve you and eliminate you from our lives?

Uh…yeah…no.

This pesky little emotion is unfortunately built into the human condition, and it's part of the human adventure. Dancing with your fear, however, can give you the greatest gifts in your life.

Fear is created by your ego. As you know now, it's your ego's job to keep you safe; therefore, the ego doesn't like to rock the boat. The ego doesn't particularly like change, unless, of course, it's going to get inflation out of the deal. In its valiant and valid effort to keep you from harm's way, the ego will use all kinds of fear tactics to ensure you remain stuck right where you are. The ego likes to play it safe, even if you're miserable. Inside your comfort zone, there is familiarity, and in that lives the illusion of safety.

I remained stuck in a job I did not love for four years, just because I was afraid. I was afraid I would be unable to do anything else. I was afraid of giving up money and stature. I was afraid of what people were going to say. I was afraid of the shame and humiliation I would feel if people judged me for walking away from a situation that many people dream of having. I was afraid of a lot of things. However, after facing my fears (which, by the way, were primarily in my head and were comprised of many limiting beliefs), I was able to transcend fear and find courage.

On the spiritual path of enlightenment, courage is a beautiful and necessary quality that infuses you with self-esteem and self-worth, and it allows you to authentically experience yourself as a divine Being.

What is fear, really? Well, according to the internet, fear is "an unpleasant emotion caused by the belief that someone or something is dangerous, likely to cause pain, or a threat." I love the first part of this: "an unpleasant emotion caused by a belief." I would also like to add that, much of the time, there is no *real* danger present. Fear is encoded in your DNA. The fight-flight-or-freeze response has been operating within the human race for thousands of years. It's this conditioned response that sends your system into "protection" mode. Since you're probably not out there killing tigers or fighting wars for your freedom, you can conclude that your conditioned response needs a little reprogramming.

Fear is what keeps you stuck. Have you ever noticed that when you feel like you're in the dark and don't know the next step, that's when you might be inclined to shut down and not even give it a try?

Mary Morrissey says, "Fear is on the fringe of familiarity." Fear does not necessarily mean there is danger; it just means you are entering an unfamiliar place. When you're calling yourself to something greater, the truth is, you've never been to this "place" before. Your ego doesn't have data in the database by which it can reference the way forward. Shine the light on this!

All of your direct experiences, and the experiences of those closest to you, formulate your belief system. These beliefs essentially get held in the database, aka your logical mind. When you make a decision to move forward in a particular direction, you check in the database to see what kind of reference material you have that will support *or* oppose the choice you have made. Your ego is an *expert* at collecting evidence that will align with your beliefs, just so it can say, "I'm right." If you can't find any evidence to support an unknown path, meaning there is no reference material in the database, fear gets activated, warning you that you are stepping outside of a place of familiarity.

Begin looking at the presence of fear simply as feedback, letting you know you are entering unfamiliar territory. This is very freeing. This awareness gives you the chance to disempower fear and move forward, even when you're "not sure" what is going to happen. The magic elixir of transforming fear into courage has enormous benefits.

Working with Fear

Have you ever noticed that when fear arises, your ability to start "dreaming up a drama" goes into hyper-mode? In about five minutes, you can imagine all of the things that could go wrong. You then conjure up in your mind—in great detail, I might add—how the tragedy will play out as well as all of the pain and suffering you are going to experience when these situations occur. Sound familiar? Can you see how this is a misuse of your incredible creative powers? This is a form of a projection. You are engaging your Life Force and giving energy to a future situation. Don't do this. When you experience fear, it's important to stay present and resist the urge to dream up a drama.

This is what I practiced repeatedly during the waiting period I went through before finding out if my former employer was going to hire me as a consultant. I stayed present, and I kept turning my focus and attention to what I wanted to create.

This is a critical time! In these telling moments, it is important for you to invest the energy that is you—your Life Force—into the possibility of what can occur in the future. While it's hard to stay fully present all the time, and while your mind can't help but wander, this is the time to start training yourself to imagine what you *do* want to happen. Try dreaming up a little dream! (A little disclaimer here: I'm not going to promise you that you're going to get exactly what you want, and if you practice this, without attachment, I can promise that you'll have a lot more fun along the way.)

When you allow your ego to be in control of your life, you dampen the feeling of aliveness of your Soul's experience. Remember, your Soul—your Higher Self, that infinite part of you—has a higher perspective on your life. This is why it's called the *Higher* Self. It will inspire you with a thought, an idea, or a dream that fills your heart with joy. In order to grow, evolve, and transform in your life, you *will* have to step outside of your comfort zone, past fear, to realize that dream.

Have you ever allowed your ego to be in the driver's seat of your life? Have you ever let this organized, logical, protective part of you talk yourself right out of your dreams, your heart's desire? Have you ever let your fear cheat you out of your aliveness? Out of creativity or expression? Out of love? When you give the ego the wheel, you diminish your own majesty and begin betraying and sabotaging your Authentic Self. Over time, if you do this enough, it will show up in your life as low self-esteem, depression, lack of self-worth, physical illness, and many other imbalances.

You have probably witnessed yourself get stuck in a negative loop in your own head. It's a downward spiral. When you are going on a rant in your own mind about all the reasons why something won't work out—how it will fail, how you will get hurt, how you will get lost, or how you will lose your money, status, or relationships—this is the voice of your ego. It's working its powers of control on you in order to keep you inside your comfort zone. It's using fear to convince you that the status quo is the only place to be. However, what I know to be true is that *no growth ever happens inside your comfort zone.*

Tip Over the Apple Cart

Do something that will upset the apple cart! Disrupt the autoplay. Move the energy! Get up and physically move around, play music, or take a walk. You can prevent the fear from taking over by placing your energy (attention/intention) somewhere else. Giving energy to the fear will cause all of the potential unfortunate scenarios to play out in your mind, and even worse, it will make you feel what it would feel like if all of these awful things *did* happen. Dr. Joe Dispenza states, "It's our feelings that literally matter." The means that the highly concentrated energy (your constant thoughts and your BIG feelings combined) actually invites the organization of molecules to conspire on your behalf. Even if something awful *were* to happen, why would you want to give it "extra time" in your life by thinking about it *before* it happens? Brené Brown, bestselling author and research professor at the University of Houston—who studies courage, vulnerability, shame, and empathy—refers to this as "dress rehearsing for tragedy."

My client Terri was estranged from her son, who had addiction issues. Long stretches of time would pass, and she would not hear from him. It was easy for her to imagine the worst. Terri wanted so badly to connect with him and to know that he was okay. She shared this with me and gave me the okay to share this with you: "I have been sending my son love with no expectations, just wishing him wellness. A few days ago, I decided to envision something more specific. I imagined him calling and saying, 'Hey, Mom, it's Dan,' and I would reply, 'Hey, Dan, how's it going?' Nothing more. I have been doing it since this weekend. Today, I got a call from Dan. I hadn't heard from him in three months. I also have to add that the call came in when I had a few minutes between meetings to check my messages; otherwise, I would have had my phone off." Terri learned to stop placing her attention on her fear. Instead, she focused her attention on what she did want, and the Universe responded. But don't take my word for it!

Connect to Your Higher Power

When you believe in a higher Infinite Intelligence, you must begin to trust that Spirit has your back. You are always receiving Higher Guidance. It's important to remember that this life is about learning. Learning asks you to push past your familiar surroundings and experience new things in your life. This is also the perfect time to call forward your authentic power as the creator you are and remember that nothing outside of you—no situation, no condition, no circumstance—will ever be greater than the authentic essence of you. Remember, the truth of your true nature is Love. Your essence is Love. You've heard this before, and I'll say it again: Choose fear, or choose love.

There is great importance in envisioning where you do want to be; it allows what you're envisioning to unfold in a way that you never could have anticipated. In a way, that is so much better! Here is what I always tell myself: "I am not smarter than God. I am not smarter than the Universe." The Universe is always unfolding with this beautiful, divine natural order and harmony. Nature is a beautiful example of this. No one is telling the grass how to grow or the birds how to fly or the flowers how to bloom. No one is "controlling" this. It simply unfolds as it's guided by this intelligent, universal Life Force. Your human body also operates according to this divine intelligence (when you take care of it).

What if you applied this idea to the unfolding of your life?

Always leave room inside for the belief that you will receive "this or something even better for the highest good of all concerned." The Universe and your own Soul's Original Wisdom are smarter than your ego-based reality. When you can shift into a knowing that things *are* unfolding for the highest good of all, it creates space for the possibility of magic to occur. You most likely often view your life from a narrow and shallow perspective. Trust that there is a grand plan. When things don't happen the way you want them to, it doesn't mean they are happening the wrong way. Trust that they are happening according to the larger overall plan that life has for you.

Trust yourself. *You* designed your life before you got here, and it's all unfolding as it should. From the Soul's perspective, there is no such thing as a misstep or failure. Your Soul is on a quest to learn. The core truth of that learning is your ability to discover and deliver to the world the truth of who you really are underneath all the patterned conditioning you've been taught. For this to unfold, you must move yourself out of your comfort zone. This is the key to coming into the fullest version of yourself and realizing your entelechy. Realizing it in Love, with Love, and as Love.

Ego Negotiation: Building a Bridge

When I quit my corporate job, I created the marketing consultant role for myself. At the time, I wasn't sure if this was what I was meant to do long-term, and it actually turned out only to be a bridge. Even though I knew I wanted to get out of hospitality, the role of consultant allowed me to significantly scale back the amount of time I was previously dedicating to the company.

On the days I wasn't working, I was restoring my health, creating a new lifestyle, and pursuing my master's degree. This happened over the course of several years. I built a bridge one step at a time. I was able to keep my ego calm about the changes I was making, because they were small changes made over time.

You can do this, too. The ego needs a bridge. It wants to be safely guided from here to there. It *needs* to feel safe. Taking small steps in the direction you want to go in is a great way to acknowledge your ego's role and purpose and then work with it to create a more expansive life. Being clear on where you are going will allow you to take steps in the direction of your highest vision. Taking small steps—one step every day—will eventually lead you to your destination. Or you will be redirected. This is the part of the process that requires the utmost amount of trust.

My husband and I regularly listen to Darryl Anka, an internationally known channeler who delivers messages from an extraterrestrial entity called Bashar. He often discusses how to live a joyful and fulfilled life. His magic formula is this: "Follow your highest excitement with no attachment to the outcome."

Did you get that? You are expanding your mind, and you're being guided by an extraterrestrial. But let's just focus on the message. The key here is to have no attachment to the outcome! This is the hard part, and this is where the magic lives.

If I had held on tightly to the path I had initially taken (become a marketing consultant), and if I had not been open to the Universe redirecting me into being a coach, you wouldn't be reading this book right now. And I would not have had this adventure or the joy of witnessing so many amazing clients shifts, nor would I have had the journey of writing this book. Again, I want to reiterate an important point: I am not smarter than the Universe. I am not smarter than what my Higher Self has planned out for my life.

The only way you can really get comfortable trusting your Higher Self is by allowing yourself to be redirected, by giving up control, and by letting your sweet self be guided.

The miracles in my life have not unfolded because I planned them. There is no possible way I am capable of even imagining the magic and miracles that are part of my beautiful life. Allowing my Higher Self to usher my ego into a new direction step by step is what built my muscle of courage. I have experienced the most amazing gifts both externally and internally. Letting go of the outcome I *thought* was best was part of the process.

The Process of Transcending Fear

Acknowledge the fear. Ignoring fear invites its relentless persistence. Like everything and everyone, it simply wants to be noticed and acknowledged. What is the worst that could happen? Could you survive that? Have you been through worse in your life and survived thus far? Would you learn something? I didn't ignore that mine was there. I nodded to it and said, "Yes, I see you, and I'm going to take this crazy step anyway, even though it doesn't make logical sense."

Recognize that fear is just information. This energetic wave of emotion is a safety call from your dear friend the ego. There is no need to assume the ego is wrong or to dismiss it. It's only doing its job and keeping you safe by encouraging you to stay inside your comfort zone and to maintain the status quo. As you begin to trust the pull of your expanded self, you can recognize you are simply receiving information.

Suspend the drama. Stay present. Come into the *now.* Pause. Resist the urge to dream up a drama about what could go wrong. Continually turn your thoughts to what you do want to happen. In my experience, this act leads you to a space of sacred learning. This is the space where you literally have the opportunity to retrain your mind, to interrupt your old patterns, and to recreate and reshape your future. The point of creation happens in the present moment. This is where possibility is birthed. It does not occur in the future or the past. If your attention is focused squarely on the future or the past, you prevent creation from having its way with you. And remember, your ego is not smarter than the Universe.

Tap into the truth. You are a divine, spiritual Being having a human adventure. The essence of you, your Spirit, is magnificent. It is so much more than anything you can even comprehend in your humanness. It *is* creation in action, and it *is* the energy of All That Is. Your Authentic Self knows this truth. The truth of you. The magnificence of you. The Original Wisdom of you. Tap into that.

Engage with life. Move toward your vision by taking action. Master coach Steve Chandler draws the distinction between information and transformation, citing that we can take in a lot of "information" from a lot of different sources, yet to experience real "transformation" life requires engagement. When you are willing to take action and engage with life, you allow yourself to be redirected, to receive information and do something with it, to learn a lesson, and to be open to feedback that tells you what works and what doesn't. Take one little step in the direction you want to go in and let life give you feedback.

Shift frustration into curiosity. Can you be present with yourself and be on your own team, believing that whatever happens is for the highest good of all concerned? Can you be excited about the possibilities of what could happen next? Are you willing to take your cues from the same infinite, organizing intelligence that guides the Universe? Can you give up control and allow yourself to be directed? Can you get curious about what is here for you to learn, to experience, and to grow into? Maybe you get frustrated when things don't happen your way or when they are not happening fast enough. Can you move into trust? Can you enjoy the moment and be open to what life wants to show you?

Raise your vibration. Gratitude is the active vibration of what you want. What I mean is that gratitude is a high human emotion. Practicing active appreciation for what you currently have in your life allows you to become the vibrational match with what you want. When you are swimming around in the lower frequency emotions, you are closer to where fear lives. Lift yourself up. Rise higher on the scale, closer to the truth of who you really are, which is Divine Love. Just by remembering this truth, you raise your consciousness and thus your vibration.

Reimagine the story you want to live. What is the experience you want to have? Where attention goes, energy flows. Place your energy on what you *do* want. Avoid giving energy to what you do *not* want. Resist giving energy to your fears. Instead, spend quality time creating the picture of what you'd love. This must first take place in your mind, in your consciousness. This picture is the energetic blueprint the Universe can use as a guide. Using your "I AM Reflection" is the perfect way to support yourself.

The Gifts Inherent in Courage

Max Lucado said, "Feed your fears and your faith will starve. Feed your faith, and your fears will." When you are willing to step out of your comfort zone, trusting the deep knowing inside that can't be defined, you open yourself up to receive many gifts. Gifts that can't be experienced in a book or collected by attending a seminar. Gifts that can only arrive through your engagement with life.

In my experience, my ability to transcend fear and find courage is what helped me alchemize all the gifts inside of me. As I walked myself through situations I couldn't have imagined, my self-esteem grew. And here's the thing: Most of us are brought up believing that our self-worth and self-esteem are derived from things outside of ourselves. We get praise for our accomplishments and achievements, and we often learn to base our worth and value on what we *do* instead of who we *are*.

No one can face your fears for you. What it's really about is how you relate to yourself while you're scared out of your mind. How you learn to trust yourself, rely on yourself, honor your choices, and love and accept all of yourself, regardless of what happens. It's about the integration of your Higher Self and your Human Self. It's you and you. You begin to get first-hand knowledge of your inherent worth, your resilience, and your majesty. You separate yourself from beliefs that no longer apply and discover the truth. You come face to face with the love that you are and the magnificence of your Being. Even writing about this is difficult, as this is not something you can really understand by

reading "information" in a book. These gifts can only be realized by stepping out of familiar territory and into the unknown,
trusting and accepting whatever happens and free-falling into
the Divine Love and magnificence that you are as your true
Authentic Self in Love, with Love, as Love.

Opportunity for Transformation
Take Action

This is the ninth Opportunity for Transformation. This is your
chance to take action and move your life forward, discover a
new part of your consciousness, and create an experience for
yourself that will deepen your learning of this material. All of
the OFTs are designed to assist you in more fully integrating
Original Wisdom from your Authentic Self into your day-to-day
life. If you would like to download an actual worksheet or listen
to an audio version of this OFT, please visit donnabond.com/
opportunityfortransformation.

Have a Little Chat with Fear

This is a journaling activity. Grab your journal and create
a safe, sacred, uninterrupted space to do some deep, quiet,
reflective work. Perhaps light a candle and put on some soft
instrumental music.

In your journal, record your answers to the following questions:

1. Is there one area in your life where you are not taking
   action because of fear?

2. Of all the possible actions you could take, can you name just one of them that you can visualize yourself making? (Remember, you're not actually doing anything yet; you are just exploring and considering it.)

3. What is the worst thing that could happen if you failed or it didn't go the way you wanted?

4. Now ask yourself, is that the worst-case scenario (that you identified in number three)? Is it something you could survive, recover from, and learn from? What kind of lessons do you believe you would learn if things didn't go your way?

5. If you could wave a magic wand and have this action produce a result you just loved, what would that look and feel like inside and outside of you?

6. What is the worst-case scenario if you *don't* take action and create change in this part of your life? What is happening on your mental, physical, emotional, and spiritual levels? If you choose not to take action and you feel the same on all levels, what do you think you might experience down the line?

7. Is this something you can be okay with? Is this something you are willing to live with?

Sacred Truth Activation

This is the ninth Sacred Truth Activation. Find a quiet, private space to center yourself, light a candle, and speak these words aloud. If you would like to listen to an audio version of this guided personal decree, please visit donnabond.com/sacredtruthactivations.

I Am Harnessing My Power as a Creator

I am a creator. I am a unique, individualized expression of the Divine. I am aware that the inspiration, enthusiasm, joy, and aliveness that flow through me are reflections of my Authentic Self, my true nature, which is pure, Divine Love. I know that when I choose love, I empower myself with the energy of creation. I know that in each moment I have the choice to focus my attention on whatever I choose. I continue to allow myself to grow, evolve, and expand as I continue on my human journey of wholeness. I am able to always choose love and reside in Love, and from there I reclaim my authentic empowerment.

When I see Love in everything and everyone, I know, understand, and recognize that I am seeing a reflection of my true Divine Self. The higher, infinite part of my true essence knows I am timeless, limitless, and eternal. I am also aware that the reason I have received inspiration is because my Soul is calling me toward fulfilling my life's purpose, which is to be in Love, with Love, and as Love in this life. Ignoring the callings of my Soul can only lead to the dampening of my Spirit and my aliveness. Because I know this, I am courageously stepping forward, trusting that I am being guided in all that I do.

I am aware that from the Soul's perspective there is no such thing as failure or mistakes. These are just definitions that have been handed down from different influences in order to explain when things are not going "my way." I am aware that many great blessings have shown themselves in my life when things did not work out according to my plan. I am open to the guidance of the Universe, and I know that everything is always unfolding with divine natural order and harmony for the highest good of all concerned.

Among the ancients, apples were believed to have magical healing properties that promote rejuvenation. As the goddess learns to love and accept herself as a human Being, she reveres the wholeness of her sweet self, which is an individualized expression of All That Is: the human and the divine. While the skin and the flesh of the apple are temporary, the apple seeds have the natural, innate, and miraculously inherent ability to regenerate infinitely. With each seed dropped into the field of infinite potentiality (with each decision she makes), she creates her reality and lives into that potential...or not. Loving all of herself and all of the journey along the way.

The fruit is produced through this mysterious process of regeneration. Its seed is filled with the same power that is within her. The goddess knows that radical acceptance of all the parts of the whole opens the gateway to other realms, providing illumination and the reclamation of her Original Wisdom. Dreaming of apples symbolizes prosperity and the goodness of life. Just as Avalon is lavishly symbolized with the apple, capturing one from the water represents crossing over into the holy isle.

Chapter Ten

Radical Acceptance
as the Path to Self-Love

"If something in your life is missing, it's probably you."

~ Dr. Robert Holden, Ph.D.

Have you ever found yourself indulging in cyclical self-care practices, believing that they were the best way to replenish yourself? If your entire life revolves around work, you may relate to what I mean. Here's what I'm talking about: You wake up thinking about work, plan your day in the shower, throw back a cup of coffee, and race into the office by 7:30 a.m., ready for your twelve-hour day. (Maybe now it's just racing down the hall to a spare bedroom or makeshift office.) You work as long as you can, eat late, and veg out in front of the TV later, absorbing some garbage that will set the stage for as much sleep interruption as possible. You come to on the couch, drag yourself to bed, pass out, wake up, and repeat. Any of this sound familiar?

Wait, there's more! On the weekends, to make up for the self-depletion and the draining of your energy resources and Life

Force, you spend most of your time employing self-care strategies, including massage appointments, haircuts and colorings, pedicures, manicures, waxing, facials, the occasional body scrub, astrology readings, and psychic readings, and if you're really needing a reboot, you've indulged in some free online webinar that turned out to be a long infomercial. Maybe you get a little exercise because you would never consider making time for these things during the busy workweek. You place all of this under the category of "self-care." After all, these were the things you needed to do in order to simply restore and revive yourself, boost your ego, temporarily feel good, and make sure you were "back to fabulous" come Monday morning.

For twenty-eight years, I honestly believed this was how it worked, until it became really clear that it wasn't.

If this resonates with you, you might be realizing these practices aren't really supporting you in a healthy, balanced way. I want to suggest that until you begin to include self-love, none of those other things will really make a difference. For me, when I was entrenched in the corporate world, self-love wasn't even something that registered in my awareness. Once I began to find compassion for myself through radical self-acceptance, there was a profound effect on my healing, and it initiated a deeper relationship with my wholeness. Radical acceptance and self-love can free you from suffering and bring you closer to your multidimensional self and the revelation that you really are a spiritual Being on a human adventure.

Radical Acceptance

"Radical acceptance" is the acknowledgement of who you are, where you've been, and where you are now. It's about profound recognition of "what is," whether your ego likes it or not. Radical acceptance includes setting aside the positions and beliefs that have caused you suffering for so long. The first step in radical acceptance is awareness, and the next step is bringing yourself into alignment with "what is." All false beliefs and self-imposed limitations simply dissolve in a moment of radical acceptance.

This act of grace occurs when you allow your Higher Self to *completely love* your Human Self. You are the only one who can do this. How? By letting go of all of your self-judgments. You let your Higher Self love your Human Self by accepting all of your "ups and downs," all of your "wins and losses," all of the "good traits and qualities" that you let everyone see, and all of the "dark and shadowy traits" that you continue to hide from everyone, including yourself. Radical acceptance is when you let your Higher Self love *all* parts of your Human Self. When you do that, you open your human heart wide enough to let your Divine Self's love envelop you. You accept and love all of you— everything—every part of your messy Human Self and every part of your clumsy, human experience. You especially love the parts you don't want to look at. When you do that, you completely embrace your wholeness. You let your Higher Self show your Human Self what it means to live in Love, with Love, and as the Love that you are. These two parts of you are not separate; you just have the illusion that they are.

The path to self-love is not found by reading a blog post or by experiencing a life-threatening illness. These can open you up to learning or to seeing new possibilities. Self-love is about *radical acceptance* of who you are, where you've been, and where you are now. It's about accepting—100 percent accepting—"what is," whether your ego likes it or not. Self-love is about setting aside *all* of the judgments of yourself, others, and life that have caused you so much suffering for so long. It's worth repeating that all suffering is derived from resistance. All resistance is created from the refusal to accept "what is."

Acknowledging that you have "positionality" about things gives you perspective. You like it "your way," and you may judge people who have a different point of view. If there is no energy charging your position, it can be viewed as a preference, so long as you don't mind if someone else has his or her own thing. If it bugs you, or really drives you crazy, it's judgment, not a preference. Your ego navigates its way through physical reality with "likes" and "dislikes." Your Authentic Self loves it all. To the Soul, it's all neutral. It just *is*.

Imagine a thousand people standing in a big circle. In the middle of the circle is a statue. As everyone looks at the statue, they each see it differently. For example, one may be looking at the front of the statue, and the person on the other side of the circle is looking at the back. Every single onlooker sees something different, yet they are all looking at the same statue. This is how life is. It just *is*.

The first step in shifting your judgment is awareness, and the next step is radical acceptance for "what is." The more you are consciously aware that you are judging, the more often you can acknowledge it and make the decision to do it less, or you can at least forgive yourself when it happens.

Finding Compassion for Yourself

My breast cancer healing journey was the beginning of the sacred act of loving myself. To me, there is a correlation between breast cancer and self-nurturance, the breast being the part of the body women use to nurture their children. At a deeper level, I also believe my cancer was related to the imbalance on my spiritual and emotional levels, and it was related to how I was dishonoring myself by not listening to or allowing my true heart's desires to be expressed in my life. I experienced having my head (the logical part of me) and my heart (the Soul part of me) out of balance. This discord resulted in my suffering (mentally, emotionally, and spirituality), and an illness showed up in my physical body.

Have you ever reflected on the idea of self-nurturing and explored what this means to you? As a driven professional trying to make it in a "man's world," have you ever even considered yourself the nurturing type? Maybe you opted out on the "kid thing" and don't have a lot of patience for children in general. Maybe you're a natural empath and you've spent a lot of time preventing your heart and your feelings from deeply connecting with other people, mostly because you don't know how to separate *your* feelings from what *other* people are feeling. As a result, this protection strategy has kept you from tuning into yourself and has caused you to remain disconnected not only from yourself but also from the people you love. Perhaps all of this prevents you from being "anywhere near" nurturing. If any of this sounds familiar, I just want to let you know I get it. I really, really get it.

Through the practice of compassionate self-forgiveness, which is taught by Drs. Ron and Mary Hulnick at the University of Santa Monica, I became aware that I was my own worst critic. Nothing was ever good enough, and I was the first one to point out my flaws. This often came across in the forms of sarcasm, putting myself down, and calling out the fact that I was wrong. I never acknowledged myself—*to* myself—for my gifts, talents, and accomplishments. It was easy to point out the talents of others since I was frequently seeking outside approval from them. When I began to examine what it meant to be self-nurturing and began to forgive myself for how badly I had treated myself, I inquired, "What's missing here? Why have I been so cruel and uncaring to myself?"

The answer was love. Love for my sweet self.

I was hit with incredible shock when I realized this. I learned at USM to view "forgiveness" from the perspective of the Higher Self, the Authentic Self. From this place, all is neutral. Everything "just is." *There is no judgment.* It's only the ego that judges, labeling everything right or wrong, good or bad. Through my journey, I learned to view life through the lens of my loving Authentic Self, which invokes the beautiful and natural process of dissolving the ego's judgments. The process is powerful and cathartic because, essentially (at least for me), I began to allow my Authentic Self to share its Loving nature and parent my humanness.

The Authentic Self has its own qualities that your ego often can't understand or comprehend. These qualities include neutrality, gentleness, joy, authenticity, acceptance, compassion, enthusiasm, aliveness, reverence, majesty, peace, and unconditional loving.

Ron and Mary teach that freedom comes when we forgive *ourselves* for ever making judgments to begin with. Because, again, from the Soul's perspective, everything is neutral. This eliminates the duality of being trapped in good or bad.

In the classroom, during the process, I spoke the following words out loud: "I forgive myself for judging myself as not taking care of myself. I forgive myself for judging myself for buying into the misbelief that my life is about hard work and sacrifice. I forgive myself for judging myself as hurting my body. I forgive myself for judging myself as getting sick. I forgive myself for judging myself as being so mean to myself. I forgive myself for judging myself for not loving myself."

It just came out. It was real and raw and shocking.

What? my mind questioned. *I don't love myself?* Compassion and deep tenderness flooded my heart. The Authentic Self part of me was present, grounded, majestic, and neutral as it supported my fragile ego in this realization. The logical me (who had just realized she was on a blind date with her Authentic Self) was stunned by the idea. *Oh my God, what did I do to myself? How did I get myself into this mess?*

The words continued to flow out of me: "I forgive myself for judging myself as treating myself so horribly. I forgive myself for judging myself as being so critical and judgmental of myself. I forgive myself for judging myself as being so critical and judgmental of everyone. For buying into the misbelief that nothing I did was good enough. For buying into the misbelief that *I* wasn't good enough. I forgive myself for judging myself as being human."

It was as if, in that moment, my Authentic Self was holding up the mirror in the gentlest, most loving, sweetest, most compassionate way, showing me what had unfolded. Reflecting to me the patterns that had led me down the path I was on. And in that moment of revelation, with the gentle assistance of my Higher Guidance, *my Soul loved my humanness.* Because I forgave the judgments I had placed on myself, I then became aware of the Love that my Divine self had *always* had for me. I had not experienced it before, as the judgments I had placed on myself had never allowed this Love to be present within me. Then the self-forgiveness opened the door for my ego to wholeheartedly love my sweet Human Self. It was truly a miracle.

In that moment, I merged more fully with my Authentic Self, and that blind date turned into a beautiful love affair. The higher part of me, my true essence, just cradled my sweet humanness, showing it compassion and gentleness and love. Like a mother would hold and comfort her child. That is the experience I was gifted with when I was willing to set aside all of the judgments of myself and arrive at the awareness that I couldn't be any more worthy of love, because I was, in fact, love itself. All of the false beliefs, misunderstandings, and self-imposed limitations simply dissolved in this moment of radical acceptance that my Human Self was ushered into by my Authentic Self. As my dear friend Robert Holden says, "It's the change that changes everything."

What Is Self-Love?

Today, I have come to know the distinct differences between self-care and self-love. And make no mistake, there is a vital difference. Self-love includes self-care, but self-care alone only skims the surface of your Beingness. Self-love is about inclusion of your wholeness on all levels—mental, emotional, physical, and spiritual. Mind, body, and Spirit.

Self-Love is about listening to your intuition and trusting yourself enough to take action. It is letting "where you are now" be okay. It is knowing that all of the answers you seek are within you. Self-love means taking some time every single day to be quiet with yourself and to acknowledge the infinite part of yourself that is connected to All That Is. It is gentle discipline. It is slowing down. It is about deeply connecting to yourself and to others. Self-love is listening to your body's needs. It is finding your voice and using it. Self-love is the acknowledgement of yourself as a divine, spiritual Being, and it's about having the awareness that you are here for a reason. It is permission to follow your joy. It is the inner knowing that you are guided and protected and that all of life is for learning. Self-love is believing in yourself. It is standing in your truth when everyone else may be telling you that you're crazy. It is listening to and being with your feelings, showing yourself an attitude of caring acceptance and compassion.

Self-love is forgiving yourself for all of it, knowing it led you to here. Self-love is realizing that in a messy, unorganized, painful, f**ked-up way, it is all really just perfect. Self-Love is radical acceptance. My personal definition of it is this: "Self-love is the honor, reverence, and compassion respecting all of the humanness and divinity that is you."

I invite you to begin self-love today. Go to a mirror. Take a long, deep look into your own eyes. Say out loud, "I love you, and I forgive you for all the things you've made wrong in your life. You didn't do anything wrong. I love and accept all of you."

For more daily practices on self-love, visit www.meetingyourselfwithlove.com.

The Soul's Perspective

From the Soul's perspective, there is no right or wrong. The Soul, your Authentic Self, is here for the experience and the lessons it can learn from the experience. As shocking as this may sound to your ego, which is often trapped in a world of right and wrong, things we see as atrocities in this human adventure are neutral to the Higher Self.

Here is a crazy idea. I think of it like this: All of humanity is essentially on what author and scholar Joseph Campbell refers to as the hero's journey. This is a story about a hero who goes on an adventure, faces adversity and crises, emerges victorious, and comes home changed and transformed. I think that is what we are all doing here. What if all of humanity is a big super-computer, and we are simply collecting data and learning from our miscreations as we continue along the path of evolution, stopping only when we arrive at a place of peace, harmony, and unity for all? And the path to get there can only be found through love. In Love, with Love, and as Love.

It's up to you to live your own hero's journey, remembering that you are a divine, spiritual Being having a human adventure.

What if none of this is real? You create your own heaven and hell here in physical reality, and what your experience is like depends greatly on your belief system and how you choose to live your life.

The ego strongly dislikes this notion because it wants to be right. Even as you read this, you may find yourself triggered. It's not comfortable to challenge your belief system. The ego likes its positionality because that's how it makes its way through the world, maintaining the *illusion* of safety, security, comfort, and control.

The Soul just accepts "what is." The Soul is here for the experience, and it has no judgment of anything in that experience. When you can shift your perceptions and move away from your positionality, you can come into acceptance with "what is." When you can do that, the resistance to what you don't like/want gets dropped, and miraculously, so does your suffering. Viola! When you forgive yourself for making something right or wrong, there is profound recognition from your Soul. You remember that you are a divine Being having a human adventure and that you're on your own path, participating in the lessons you need to learn from life's adventures. When you forgive yourself for your judgments, the Soul part of you—the infinite part, the higher part of your essence—remembers that we are all One. When you can let go of your judgments of yourself and others, a powerful healing takes place, and your natural state of loving is revealed. In the process of releasing your judgments, you become compassionate, realizing you are just doing the best you can. This cathartic and revolutionary process, which I've had the privilege of learning about at the University of Santa Monica, sets you free from your self-created suffering and gives you the incredible feelings of freedom, peace, and revelation.

Freedom from Suffering

While it seems like forgiving the other person is the sensible thing to do, Drs. Ron and Mary teach that when you do that, there is still part of you that is saying the other person is wrong. When you maintain the ego position, which believes that there is right and wrong, you continue to hold on to your judgments, and consequently, you continue to suffer. The Soul is here for the experience only, and the Soul has no opinion about how it gets the experience it's looking for.

Another way to view your judgments is to see them as accusations. And because you live in a world that reflects everything that is going on in your own consciousness back to you, when you judge someone else, for whatever it is, you are really judging yourself. Do unto others… You know the saying. It's not just do good and get good, though. Whatever you do (or say or think, for that matter), you are really doing to yourself. Life is a hall of mirrors.

Accepting that we are all one is really an incentive to see everyone and everything through the eyes of Love.

There is something magical about this process, which is taught by Drs. Ron and Mary. When I first learned how to forgive myself for my own self-imposed judgments, it seemed mechanical. I talked through the process, and it seemed rote and inauthentic. I continued to work with self-forgiveness. I got better at it. Finally, I saw it as powerful and freeing. This happened when I really *felt the judgments* in my heart, took 100 percent responsibility for them, and intentionally *decided* that I would let them go.

Acceptance is the antidote to all of your suffering. The way I understand it, when you can cooperate with the way things are, all resistance drops and all of your self-imposed suffering does, as well. When you are able to move into a place of acceptance, believing that "it is what it is" without having to label anything as right or wrong, you experience incredible freedom.

In many spiritual texts and literature, forgiveness is highlighted as a spiritual undertaking. Drs. Ron and Mary have taken this idea a step further by encouraging us to see our judgments through a spiritual lens, through our Higher Selves, from the perspective of our spiritual Beingness, the place where we are all one. In that, the grievances we hold can just simply dissolve. To do this, you must be ready to take responsibility for the experiences you are having in your life.

Radical Acceptance of Your Humanness

In the process of radical acceptance, you come to terms with your humanness. When you move away from your positionality and stop getting caught up in right and wrong, you can, in a way, lay down the sword, stop the fight, and align with a beautiful and mystical truth: We are all just human. Being human can be messy. As you radically accept *all* the parts of yourself (and everyone else), you can begin to transfer that loving essence of the truth of who you are to *all* the parts of you, messy or not. In this practice of self-love, you begin to fall in love with your wholeness.

Your wholeness includes your multidimensionality; that higher, infinite, majestic, grand, wisdom-filled part of your essence; *and* your messy, judgmental, critical, ego-based way of seeing the world. Moving into an inner place of loving acceptance for *all* the parts of you is the only way you can begin to transform. You can't get to "over there" until you are first willing to meet yourself where you are. Coming into radical acceptance of yourself *and* everyone else, accepting that "they are who they are," allows you to connect with your divine self. When you experience this, you move forward and create a different life, a more beautiful life, for yourself. From here, you begin to see and acknowledge all of the blessings around you. With each of life's experiences, you realize that gifts and lessons are always present for you, giving you the opportunity to evolve. When you have compassion and love for yourself and the world, you are then grateful for all of life's unfolding.

Opportunity for Transformation
Take Action

This is the tenth Opportunity for Transformation. This is your chance to take action and move your life forward, discover a new part of your consciousness, and create an experience for yourself that will deepen your learning of this material. All of the OFTs are designed to assist you in more fully integrating Original Wisdom from your Authentic Self into your day-to-day life. If you would like to download an actual worksheet or listen to an audio version of this OFT, please visit donnabond.com/opportunityfortransformation.

Radical Acceptance Exercise

Close your eyes, take a deep breath, and be fully present within yourself. Remember, you are a unique, individualized expression of the Divine. Consciously tune into your Essential Nature, the loving presence that you are. From this place, answer these questions in your journal:

1. Call to your awareness a recent situation in which you were experiencing resistance (due to positionality) in the form of judgment, expectation, or attachment. What was occurring, and what were you experiencing?

2. Get really honest with yourself and write down how you may have imposed your stance on the situation and, in turn, created resistance for yourself.

3. As you remember the truth of who you are and consider the possibility that life is always unfolding in divine, natural order and harmony, are you willing to consciously let go of your position (which may include your bias, agenda, opinion, or prejudice) and see the situation from the perspective of your Soul?

4. How could this situation be providing you with an opportunity to grow, learn, and evolve into your next level of expansion?

5. From a place of inner neutrality, as you come to accept "what is" and begin to view the situation from a place of radical acceptance, write in your journal any inner shifts you are experiencing or Original Wisdom you are aware of.

When you have completed the exercise, acknowledge yourself *out loud* and give yourself credit for being willing to demonstrate loving acceptance and to see perfection in All That Is. Complete this exercise any time you find yourself struggling with judgment or feeling resistance in a situation.

Sacred Truth Activation

This is the tenth Sacred Truth Activation. Find a quiet, private space to center yourself, light a candle, and speak these words aloud. If you would like to listen to an audio version of this guided personal decree, please visit donnabond.com/sacredtruthactivations.

I Am Seeing Perfection in All That Is

In my life, I will encounter people, situations, and circumstances that may not be the way I want them to be or the way I think they should *be. I am aware that when I bring my positionality to a situation and* force *my way upon something, I create resistance and, essentially, my own suffering.*

I am clear in my knowing that moving out of reactivity and resistance and into acceptance is the process of coming into alignment with "what is." I am in cooperation and am willing to drop my stance and come into full acceptance of whatever is unfolding, regardless of whether or not it is my preference to do so. I acknowledge that this is a growth and learning opportunity for my ego, and in this moment I release my investment in right and wrong. I am clear that the spiritual perspective recognizes that all is perfect just the way it appears to be. I trust that Divine Intelligence is at work.

I am aware that while on my Soul's journey, I am receiving what I need for my continued growth, learning, and expansion. I am aware that life is always unfolding in divine, natural order and harmony for the highest good of all concerned.

I am open to understanding, on a deeper level, from the Soul's perspective, that perfection exists in all things and that my Higher Self is here for the experience. When I am residing in the love that I am, and when I view life's unfolding through the lens of my Soul, I invite myself to see perfection in All That Is.

After her adventure, the goddess rests in the sacred place that has always been. She just didn't recognize it until now. Changed forever by her passage into the Apple Land of Eternal Life, she has healed her wounds and is reflecting on how each unique step she traveled was instrumental in leading her to the grand crescendo: her recognition of her divine self. She weeps with deep and profound gratitude for the mystery of the entire unfolding. Magical apples of immortality are symbolic of death and rebirth. It is through her life's entire journey, her rebirth, and her awakening that the goddess's powers are harnessed in the expression of her whole human and divine self.

It is in the realization of her power along the path, through gratitude and grace, that she acknowledges and reclaims her greatest gifts, the pinnacle being the revelation of her true Authentic Self and the knowing that we come for it all. Our gifts are not received upon our arrival at the destination; they are gathered like gemstones throughout the journey.

Chapter Eleven

Gratitude is Everywhere You Want to Be

"Our purpose for being alive is fulfilled by moving
more and more deeply into our Spiritual hearts
and experiencing the presence of Love."

~ Drs. Ron and Mary Hulnick

I was first able to reside in the Love that I am and have a deep, profound, visceral feeling of gratitude for my humanness and my life on the very last day of the Consciousness, Health, and Healing portion of my master's in Spiritual Psychology. (This third year of the master's program was supposed to be my last class, but of course, I went on to "year four" to earn my Soul-Centered Coaching certification.) It was the last morning of the six-day lab, an intense, collaborative study that was designed to infuse a higher consciousness in one's life. It was the culmination of all of the teachings of the previous ten months. I looked at it as the opportunity to literally embody the qualities of the Authentic Self—which Ron and Mary define as Compassion,

Honesty, Acceptance, Authenticity, Joy, Peace, Unconditional Love, and Gratitude—and then merge them with my ego.

Having—and practicing—gratitude will not only raise your vibration, attracting positive energy into your life; it will also increase your awareness of the beautiful synchronicities you encounter. When you are residing in a place of gratitude, you become more cognizant of the many gifts that surround you and the miracles that unfold in your life with the purpose of increasing your joy and deepening your connection to your Authentic Self. The more you appreciate all of the abundance in your life, the more you will naturally continue to experience it.

Unfolding My Wings

On this last day of class, I woke up and felt aches and pains all over. There was hot, burning fire between my shoulder blades and a dull, hard ache in my heart space. I used the lab process to explore this physical pain. I was aware that all of these aches that had been plaguing me were directly connected to the withholding of the love in my heart. By God's grace and my willingness to let go and let God, which I had practiced with vigilance during this lab, I was able to experience an opening of the heart that was profoundly visceral. I felt a "letting go" like none other, a lifting that was deep and full and profound. As the upheaval was dislodging from my chest, I fell back into my chair, my arms outstretched and my heart pointing to the heavens, offering myself up to God for healing. Surrendering...surrendering. I felt cradled, supported, and loved in that chair, as if I were being held in the hand of the Divine. This support and the loving space I was in with my trio mates, Ed and Elsie, allowed me to continue releasing and letting go.

It felt as if a train of energy were pouring out of my chest, releasing years of withholding, contraction, and control. It just kept releasing and releasing as I continued to surrender at a deeper and deeper level. I was unsure if I was still inside my physical frame or if I was now merged with and part of everything and everyone. When the release of this energy had calmed, I felt a tiny wind, a small breeze blowing out of my back, going out between the middle of my shoulder blades and going through the middle of my heart space. I was aware that my heart was now open—exploded open—more than it had ever been in this life. This calm and apparent stream of loving energy continued pulsating through my heart space and out my back. It felt like a gentle stream.

Following that, I experienced a deep and profound peace, something I can only describe as the Love of God. I was given the vision of a drop of water in a still pond, with the ripples moving outward. I saw a lotus flower off to the side. I experienced a sense of oneness and stillness like never before.

Later that same day, the afternoon trio proved equally magnificent, and this time I worked with the idea of "withholding." I explored the potential gifts that were available to me if I was willing to sacrifice some of the patterns I had grown accustomed to. I looked at how, in the past, I had been withholding sharing parts of myself in the form of always "keeping it in check." I had a flashback to my first year in class at USM. Mary Hulnick had told me to go out and play in the mud. Suddenly, two and a half years later, I finally understood what she meant. As I examined this now clearly obvious pattern in my life, I felt shocked that I had never seen it before. I immediately knew that "keeping things in check" was 100 percent connected to the physical body pain I had been constantly experiencing in my life. As I went through the release process, I had a lot of energy and emotion around these ideas. I dug deep and verbally articulated my heartfelt prayer to Spirit, asking to be released from my withholding. "Please release this pattern of 'keeping it in check,'" I said.

At the start of every process at USM, the words "invoke your inner counselor" are said. For the past year and a half, each time I had heard these words, I had received an image of my huge, glorious, angel-type wings rising. They were always positioned above me and were beautifully strong. And what I never noticed before this trio, before this surrender, was that my wings *were always folded up*. They were held tightly together, pulled in, folded up. Kept in check.

Suddenly, in another divine moment of revelation, while letting go and letting God, my arms went back, and my heart shone up to the gods, and my wings unfolded. These enormous, beautiful, white-feathered wings, like the wings of a white dove, were finally freed. They unfurled as I realized that all of the pain in my shoulders, neck, and upper back was directly linked to my containment of me, which was represented by these incredible wings. In that moment, all was released. I let go and let God, and I experienced greater freedom in an even more profound and visceral way than I had earlier that morning. All of my physical discomfort dissolved instantly in that release, and I physically felt completely unrestrained and full of love and aliveness.

My wings spanned and filled the entire Brentwood Ballroom, where class was being held. My wings acted as a nurturing cover, sheltering all the other Souls with Love and Light, as they each experienced their own process of letting go. From this moment on, for the rest of the lab and the remaining trios, each time I invoked my inner counselor, these massive, gorgeous, majestic wings were now set free. And even now, my wings continue to gracefully preside over my life and all of my adventures.

Free at last.

As I reflected upon this, I was reminded of the beginning of my journey, when I was on an airplane, feeling throbbing pain in my shoulder and encountering the poem "Risk":

Risk
And then the day came,
When the risk
To remain tight
In a bud
Was more painful
Than the risk
It took
To blossom.

And in that moment, I knew I had come full circle. I had completed a divine healing journey that had placed me back at the beginning, centering me in the true understanding of who I am as a divine Being having a human adventure. And I felt profound gratitude for the fact that I had had an experience of my own divinity and for the fact that I was able to reclaim my own authentic power in my humanness.

Blessings Abound

I am grateful for my breast cancer—for the healthy changes it prompted me to make in my life, for the discoveries I made about myself, and for the compassion I learned to have for myself.

I learned to love and revere myself as a Divine Being on a human adventure. As I reflect over my life, I feel deeply grateful, as I now see how all of it makes sense. At the time, it had been easy to feel trapped by things that were not working out for me, and there is always a reason why life unfolds as it does.

When I was the West Coast VP of sales and marketing for a hospitality management company back in 2007, there was a sales contest, and if we won, the top sales professionals would be sent on an all-expenses-paid trip to Cancun, Mexico. As the leader of the entire Western region, I made my budgeted numbers that year and generated lots of profit and market share earnings for the company. Well, the East Coast guy achieved his numbers, too. And they were just slightly ahead of mine. He went to Cancun, not me.

I was so mad! Given how small our organization, given the fact that there was just the two of us, and given the fact that I had plenty of salespeople who had accomplished the goal and were going on the trip, I could *not* understand why I wasn't permitted to go to Cancun. It seemed ridiculous. I was deeply rooted in my "positionality," and I couldn't stop thinking of all the reasons why I thought I should go. And when I didn't get to go, I suffered emotionally. This went on for months, as there was an entire quarter between the year-end results and the trip!

That week, when almost *everyone* at the company was in Cancun—except our administrative assistant, HR, and me—I went out on a blind date. The guy on the date just happened to be in SoCal *for that week only*, as he was from out of town. Today, that guy is my husband.

After the fact, it's super easy to be grateful and appreciate that I didn't go on that trip. And I could have saved myself a lot of heartache if I had been more tuned into potential blessings that would come. I could have been calmer *if* I had known the Universe "had my back."

That's the choice you are given whenever something happens. You get to choose your perspective on everything in life. And it's that perspective, from moment to moment, that shapes your entire world. It's the moments together that make up your life. How great it is to understand that the one thing you are actually in control of is how you look at things!

The Frequency of Gratitude

Everything you want is in the frequency of gratitude. Bringing gratitude into your everyday experience allows you to reside in the highest vibrational frequencies—on the high end of the scale, close to the truth of who you really are, which is the energy of Love. The more time you spend on that high vibrational level of loving and gratitude, the more you will manifest what you desire in life. It may not look exactly how you want it to look, and the Law of Magnetic Attraction is always working. The expression of gratitude includes reverence, revelation, joy, and completeness.

To activate and maintain this frequency, practice gratitude in your life daily. When you're in the midst of something you do not enjoy and can still demonstrate gratitude *in* the experience and gratitude *for* the experience, that means you are well on your way to matching this high frequency in your everyday life. This is where you invite in the belief that *everything that is happening in life is happening for you*. It's all perfect for you and your journey. The experiences and the lessons your Soul came here to experience.

Gratitude is the vibrational energy and the doorway to receiving abundance. It is a primary ingredient of a happy life. Gratitude is a higher vibration than even joy, because to feel grateful you need to feel contentment, which is defined as a joyful state of being. The joy comes first, and then the gratitude is a step higher.

The natural and universal law of receiving is activated through the act of giving. A key factor of giving, however, is that it will only activate the law of receiving when it is done with no expectation of anything in return. When you are in a state of gratitude, it's a natural state of giving thanks. When done from love—with a genuine, open heart and no expectations—the law of receiving is automatically activated. Being in a consistent state of gratitude throughout all the moments of your life allows you to receive more of what you want.

When you view your life from the Soul's perspective, you can see the perfection in all experiences—in the perceived good and bad. Success and failure are just definitions that we humans make up. The Soul is neutral. It's here for the experience, regardless of what it is or how we label it in our humanness. Many perceived "failures" lead to places you would not have gotten to otherwise. Being grateful for everything that is happening opens the door for you to see your life as the beautiful unfolding of perfection. A grand tapestry.

Believing that even a seemingly "negative" situation that you are in will ultimately conclude with a "positive" result allows you to shift the energy and your vibration so that you will always attract a beneficial result. When you begin to see the world this way, it becomes a self-fulfilling prophecy.

Using Active Appreciation as a Strategy

With every thought you have, an emotional response will follow. Thoughts *always* precede emotions. Every thought impacts your emotional state. Moment by moment, you choose which thoughts to entertain and invest energy in, and predictable emotions follow.

Emotions with a higher frequency—such as love, peace, and joy—are what we are all seeking. When you're in love and you feel joy, you feel lighter and more uplifted, and you are filled with clarity and inspiration. Things seem to go your way. You easily see opportunities and new possibilities. You experience being "in the flow."

One of the quickest, most powerful ways to raise into the higher emotional realms is by being appreciative. It is different than gratitude, which comes with a feeling of having overcome something or achieved something associated with it. The expression of appreciation is a powerful positive activation *now*. When you are upset or are in a difficult situation in your life, it's not always easy to maintain a sustained level of love, joy, and gratitude, and you can *always* find things to appreciate. The chair under your bottom, the sleeping cat by your side, the view out the window, or the water in your glass. Appreciation can be used as a tool to intentionally guide your thoughts and raise your emotional vibration, lifting you to where love, joy, and peace reside. Actively practicing appreciation in the difficult moments places you back in the stream of expansion rather than contraction. It takes you higher. The more time you spend appreciating, the more you encounter uplifted emotions and the experiences that are a vibrational match to them.

You can choose which thoughts to entertain and invest energy in every day. When you have a negative thought, you can choose to interrupt it. In doing so, you bypass the resulting negative emotion and the potential physical experience. Momentarily stopping and appreciating something—anything—in that moment can be an effective tool to shift negative thinking.

Therefore, your role is to *be* what you want to match with. If you want to experience more love, joy, happiness, and peace, *be* in those emotional states. Look for evidence of these states in your life and appreciate them. Whatever emotional state is most dominant becomes the light post that brings forth more experiences that reflect the state you are in.

Integrating Active Appreciation into Your Life

My husband and I taped a piece of paper to the inside of the bathroom medicine cabinet. Every day, we write something we appreciate. In the past, I have written the high thread count of my sheets, a butterfly going by, my amazing clients and the incredible shifts they are having, my kitty-cats, and the silver in my hair. My husband has written our garden, great surfing, a good hair day, listening to music, and creating brilliant works in his art studio.

What are you appreciating? Blessings are everywhere. Notice them. Look at your money, relationships, health, family, career, beloved pets, and surroundings and notice all of the beauty in each of these areas. Be in a state of appreciation for all of the many blessings that surround you. They are everywhere. You just need to slightly shift your attention and notice them.

If you look at your money, for example, and you allow your first thought to be that "it's not enough," *that* becomes the active vibration you resonate with. "Not enough" then gets "matched" because of the Law of Attraction, and you stay in the loop of not-enoughness. Give your money some love. Appreciate all of the things it does do for you. Offer active appreciation for what is in your experience and see what happens when you become the match to that.

Ponder and savor what you place your attention on. Revel in the many wonderful things you have going on around you at any moment. Slow down. Take a deep breath and appreciate. There is plenty of goodness to find. Get closer. It is there. This simple practice can transform your life. Joy is all around, hidden in everything. You will see that easily when you begin an active practice of appreciation and gratitude.

Each morning, my alarm sounds from across the room. I have to get out of bed to shut it off. I do this to wake myself up and to make sure I'm not tempted to hit the snooze button, roll over, and go back to sleep. But I do get back in bed for a few minutes and move into feelings of gratitude and appreciation. I appreciate the soft, warm bed that is supporting my body. I am grateful for my husband's warm, beautiful body, which is lying next to mine. I appreciate the two cats in the window as they chirp at a hummingbird feeding outside. I am grateful for the roof over my head and for the eclectic furniture in my bedroom. I lie there for a few minutes, just feeling the peace of the silence. The stillness of the morning. The breath and the energy pulsing through my physical body. For all that, I am grateful. Grateful for this life and for all of my experiences in it. For the journey. For the mystery, the wonder, the miracles, and the love.

I then get up; go to the bathroom; feed my cats, Mystic and Rumi; and then sit down in my meditation space. I spend a few more minutes being grateful for whatever is happening outside my window, be it the clouds or the sky or the California sunshine streaming in. Sometimes it's a hawk or the orange sun pushing its way into the day. I actively appreciate the plants in our yard, which my husband has nurtured and cared for. Every day, this is the first part of my practice. *Being* grateful. I just want to point out I'm not "doing" anything here.

Opportunity for Transformation
Take Action

This is the eleventh Opportunity for Transformation. This is your chance to take action and move your life forward, discover a new part of your consciousness, and create an experience for yourself that will deepen your learning of this material. All of the OFTs are designed to assist you in more fully integrating Original Wisdom from your Authentic Self into your day-to-day life. If you would like to download an actual worksheet or listen to an audio version of this OFT, please visit donnabond.com/opportunityfortransformation.

Active Appreciation Exercise

Buy yourself a small journal and keep it by your bedside. For at least thirty-three days (or the rest of your life, if you prefer), upon awakening, write down several things you appreciate in the moment. It could be the sound of your children in the house, your pet delivering unconditional love, the good feelings in your body, the warmth of your sheets, a cherished relationship, or the anticipation of something you have planned that day. Some things on your list might repeat from day to day. And you'll find that the more you observe, the more there is to appreciate. Do this every morning for at least a month and watch how profoundly your life transforms.

Gratitude Review

Get quiet. Look back over your life. Identify a difficult time or experience you've endured. Perhaps it was something you perceived as a failure, or maybe it was trauma, drama, or tragedy in your life. Journal about it and answer these questions:

What gifts came out of this experience? In other words, what do you have today that is a result of that difficult experience? Can you see the growth you've experienced as a result of this event, though you may have labeled it as "bad" at the time? What blessings are you aware of that are in your life because of what happened?

Sacred Truth Activation

This is the eleventh Sacred Truth Activation. Find a quiet, private space to center yourself, light a candle, and speak these words aloud. If you would like to listen to an audio version of this guided personal decree, please visit donnabond.com/sacredtruthactivations.

I Am Appreciative of and Grateful for All of My Life

I am aware that when I lose my center or when I am in a stuck place, I can slow down, become fully present, and move into the active state of being appreciative. I am able to appreciate everything. In this state, I move past judgment, and I move into acceptance of what is. I lovingly bring my attention to what is happening around me. I acknowledge and notice everything. I gently and silently bring my focus, attention, awareness, and energy to the endless surroundings that permeate my consciousness. In that, I give my thanks. I am grateful for what is. I am in a space of active appreciation. I marvel at my thoughts of apprecia- tion, and I stay in this space long enough to mentally, emotionally, and physically experience a shift in my energy. In this active vibration, I am able to notice and appreciate things I may have previously overlooked.

I am grateful for everything in my life. I am grateful for all of the experiences I have had and all of the experiences that I am yet to have. As I move into a space of gratitude, I am able to experience the deep well of abundant Love that springs up from my inner essence, and I am aware of the many blessings in my life. I am deeply grateful for all of my relationships—the ones that are harmonious and the ones that are presenting me with the opportunities for growth and learning. I am grateful for all of my circumstances, conditions, and situations, including the ones I enjoy, the ones that feel supportive of me and in alignment with me, and the ones that are presenting me with my next opportunity for healing, growth, and expansion. I am grateful for all of it. I am able to cultivate active appreciation and to be aware that it is always possible for me to shift. I am grateful for my decision to be filled with the flow of appreciation and the abundance of gratitude. I am pausing in this place to be still and know that I Am.

Geoffrey of Monmouth, author of Vita Merlini *(Life of Merlin), written circa 1150, said, "The island of apples, which is called fortunate, is truly named, for it brings forth all things of its own accord. It needs no farmers to till the fields, and there is no cultivation save that which nature provides. It freely brings forth fertile stalks and grapes, and apples born of precious seed in its forests. The earth nourishes all things, as bounteous as tended land; one lives there a hundred years or more."*

Fortunate gets its name because it produces all things of itself. In the same way, the whole journey itself is the realization that we are the Love that we seek. The Isle of Avalon, as one of the possible resting places of the Holy Grail, is the symbolic paradise of Beingness that we come to know in the unfolding entelechy of each one of us. For eons of time, humans have outwardly pursued the treasure of the sacred Holy Grail, not realizing the whole time that they are really in search of themselves. The mystery is perhaps in the paradox between the "real world" of the legend and the "spiritual world" of the myth. Now is the hour for humanity to awaken, to realize, and to stop looking out there for what we think we want. It is time to begin looking within, at the magnificence of who we are. We are so much closer than we think.

Chapter Twelve

The Process Is the Point

"We are travelers on a cosmic journey, stardust swirling
and dancing in the eddies and whirlpools of Infinity. Life
is Eternal. We have stopped for a moment to encounter each
other, to meet, to love, to share. This is a precious moment.
It is a little parenthesis in eternity."

~ Paulo Coelho

In October of 2015, a few days before my husband and I left for a trip to the UK, I received a shamanic healing in which I received Soul Retrieval and Power Animal Retrieval. In shamanic tradition, a Power Animal Retrieval is a method used to connect us to helping Spirits who show themselves in the form of animals. These helping Spirits can provide us, our families, our communities, and even an organization or country with power, protection, and support. I learned my power animal is a white dove named Cari.

Finding out my power animal is a dove became an important and meaningful part of my journey. It helped me to realize *that each step along the way informs what will happen next.* As you strengthen the relationship with your Authentic Self, you will begin to realize that the way you're being guided on the journey is part of the rich learning your Soul has in store for you. As long as you are alive, what may appear as a final destination is really just a pivot point to the next part of the journey. When you are focused on the pivot point, you overlook the gifts being offered in the present moment, and you miss the lesson. You miss the point.

My Journey to the Land of Apples

We arrived in Glastonbury, England. Our trip was driven by synchronicity. First, Paul has a tattoo of the sacred geometry symbol Vesica Piscis, which are two interlocking circles adorned with vines and florals. This symbol—which is on his lower torso, tucked under his clothing—exactly matches the famous Chalice Well cover of the Red Springs in Glastonbury. Second, I grew up in a town called Glastonbury, not the one in England, but the one in the state of Connecticut. It was these synergistic connections that invited us into the mystery that awaited us.

What we didn't know at the time was this: The Chalice Well lid, featuring the Vesica Piscis, was designed by the Abbey Church architect and archaeologist Frederick Bligh Bond (Uh, yes…Bond. As in Donna Bond) and was presented as a gift after the Great War in 1919. The symbol also has a sword bisecting the two interlocking circles (as does Paul's tattoo). Some say it's a possible reference to Excalibur, the sword of the legendary King Arthur, which is believed to be buried at the Glastonbury Abbey. As the legend goes, King Arthur placed the Holy Grail, for safe-keeping, in the hands of Joseph of Arimathea, who is rumored to have buried it at the bottom of the Chalice Well on the Isle of Avalon, known today as Glastonbury, England.

We specifically traveled to Glastonbury to see the Chalice Well and to climb the famous Tor, which is an English hillside located in Somerset, topped by a monumental tower that was erected in honor of St. Michael.

Or at least that's why we thought we were there.

As soon as we arrived, my highly attuned husband looked me in the eye and announced, "We are going to the Abbey."

I thought, *I didn't even know there was an Abbey.*

We meandered through the incense-scented town of Glastonbury, which was a short walk from our little bed and breakfast, and went to the Abbey. We paid for our entrance tickets and passed through the gate, and right before crossing onto the actual grounds, we stopped at a statue of a monk on a donkey. He was looking down at a child who was holding up an apple. I noticed it but didn't really give it that much thought until we were on our way back out. Truthfully, at the time, it didn't really register that the child was extending his hand, offering an apple.

Paul and I continued on our way toward the ancient ruins. I was immediately enveloped in a beautiful, peaceful energy. It was warm and soft and seemed to be cradling us. We first walked into the tiny St. Patrick's chapel, where we lit a candle and wrote a prayer. I prayed that our love would last forever and that we would live in joyful happiness together always. I left my little prayer note in a basket under the altar.

We left the chapel and stumbled upon the first of the ruins. Before we even entered what is known as The Lady Chapel, Paul and I had a powerful feeling of remembering and familiarity. He fell to his knees and wept. I experienced a profound sense of

Love and oneness with Paul. Together, we walked into The Lady Chapel, which featured beautiful, majestic corner archways that were missing their walls but that stood gracefully, holding in the history. Paul pointed up to a rustic open-arch ledge, and resting on it was a single white dove. I giggled in disbelief at first, but then my breath was taken away as a second white dove snuggled up to the first, and they both looked down lovingly at Paul and me for a long time, almost as if to say, "Welcome back."

I burst into tears of love and joy and gratitude. I was enfolded in the warmth of profound Love, and I allowed it to pour out of me. I was transcended to another time and place, although I was unsure of where and when. I felt memories flooding into me, although I was unable to make any logical sense of what was happening. It was as if time was standing still and eons of time and history were merging with my Beingness. I was so overcome with emotion that I was unable to control it. I broke down in deep, guttural sobs and let it all flow out. For the next twenty minutes or so, we communed in harmony with those doves. I was with God. We were with God. It was a cleansing and an awakening and a merging with the most profound Love and grace I had ever experienced. Little did I know, this was just a blossom of what was in store for me.

It was the late afternoon, and the sun was setting, casting the most beautiful magical glow on the grounds of the Abbey. We were in deep reverence and awe of the extraordinary healing we experienced. Appreciating the beauty of all that was happening, we let ourselves be enfolded in all the love and beauty that surrounded us. We meandered outside and walked around the beautiful grounds as the sun sparkled and as thick, expansive, green-blanketed lawns folded into one another. We moved gracefully over the lawns, drinking in the beauty of the setting sun and the deep peace.

We were brimming with the knowing that somehow, in some faraway time centuries ago, we had shared a life together, and it was somehow tied to this sacred land. In my heart, I had always known that Paul was "home" for me, but on this day we were gifted with the Soul recognition that we had indeed shared a life together. And we were both tied to the Abbey in some way. Perhaps we had lived in the ancient lost land of Avalon, the Isle of Apples. The random clues of Paul's tattoo and the name of my childhood hometown had guided us there. In the moment Paul and I had reconnected in this life, we had fallen in Love, and we had always known we had a deep, soulful connection beyond words. On this glorious day, September 30, 2015, we were reminded of this powerful Soul connection in the most extraordinary way.

We wandered aimlessly around the beautiful grounds, and it was as if every tree, every leaf, every blade of grass, every stone, and every bug was connected to us, welcoming us back, welcoming us home.

We sat on a bench. The place where we sat overlooked the grave where King Arthur and Guinevere had been laid to rest hundreds of years before. We thought about the legend of the lost land of Avalon and the buried Holy Grail. In the corner, by a ruin stone, we looked down into the tall grass and saw a single apple lying there. *Really?* It was a fleeting thought to myself and then we continued on our way.

Paul was ahead of me with the camera. He was like a kid in a candy store, following the allure of the magical, dancing light. I followed at my own pace. We each had our own experience that day, in addition to profound moments we had had with those two love doves.

I happened along a pond with water lilies. It was lovely, but it was hard to make it out very well, as the sun was shining right into my eyes, causing my sight to be distorted. As I gazed at the water lilies and flowers in this pond, I noticed that, floating around the edges of this moat, there appeared to be *many* apples bobbing along the edges. *What? Really?* I thought. *I must be seeing things.* Since the Universe had brought me an apple in the form of that elaborate dessert, it seemed quite serendipitous that there would be apples floating in this pond. It actually seemed kind of ridiculous. In fact, it was ridiculous in the most unbelievable way. It made no sense that there were apples floating here!

Paul started motioning to me. I walked into what I thought was a forest and saw my husband standing there, the most beautiful look of musing on his face. I took in the beauty of him—this extraordinary man who had found me on the worldwide web. I lovingly gazed at him, wanting to lock eyes, but his were darting back and forth between me and the ground below us.

I looked down and was met with the shocking realization that there were literally hundreds of apples on the ground. Hundreds! Shock and awe rose within me as I lifted my gaze and discovered that I was standing under an apple tree. An apple tree which was abundantly pregnant and bursting with ripe, sweet, bright-red fruit. I could not believe the experience I was having. In that moment, the gift of my Spirit called me to my knees, and I allowed the tears to flow down my face. I allowed my heart to be overjoyed, overfilled with pure, Divine Love and gratitude. Again. This day was pure magic. Pure Spirit-filled magnificence as I communed with the Universe, with Source, and with God. I lifted my sight to the next tree and the next one and the next one, only to realize I was kneeling in the middle of an abundantly rich apple orchard.

We laughed and cried. Paul took pictures of me among a pile of apples under the most beautiful, expectant apple tree I'd ever seen. There we were, in the middle of a magical orchard that I believed to be behind the veil in the miraculous lost land of Avalon, hidden behind the Glastonbury Abbey.

This life is filled with miracles and magic. What if you could be open to the wonder? Can you believe that magic is actually possible, and can you invite it into your life? Can you trust that when you do, there it is?

This was also a loud and clear message from the Universe that *I am so much more than what I've believed until now.* The symbol of the apple, for me, has become a nod from the Universe, and it tells me that I am on the right track and that I am following the correct line of breadcrumbs.

Paul joked with me about being a supreme manifester as he snapped away with his camera, capturing and documenting more of the magic of that day. We laughed, and we cried. We stared deep into each other's eyes, letting our hearts pour out the most profound love and gratitude, as we allowed the loving presence of our Souls to embrace us.

We then heard bells ringing, and we kissed. (Since our honeymoon in Italy, whenever we hear bells, especially church bells, we stop what we are doing and kiss. Corny? You better believe it. That's what happens when you're living in a fairy tale. You get to believe whatever you want to believe.)

It was six o'clock. The Abbey keeper was walking through the orchard, gently ringing a handbell. The Abbey was closing for the day. This rustic man came up to us. His long, wiry hair and nest-like beard beautifully represented a man who lived as the keeper of the Abbey. I stood, looking into his Soul, and said, "Thank you. This is the most beautiful place I have ever been to on the planet." I was not shy. I did not hold back my tears. He looked at me with a tiny bit of remorse, sad that he had to send us away, and he seemed to understand, at least in some small way, the miracle that occurred.

The Journey Is the Destination

My whole life, I have been discovering my Original Wisdom through what I call "taking the journey in." Nothing else in my life has been more fulfilling, more joyful, richer, more rewarding, more magical, and just plain *more* than the uncovering and discovering of my Authentic Self. Ever since I was young, I have always been fascinated with and in love with the mystery of the Universe, the mystery of me, and the mystery of how my small role somehow fits into the overall grand plan.

For a long time, my life was the quest of finding a destination. In my twenties and thirties, I searched for the love of my life. At forty, I found my soulmate, and still the void remained. After my early twenties, I searched for my life's purpose; I had always been searching. In the physical world, so many of us chase things we think are going to make us happy—a relationship, a job, a house, a car, more money. I chased all of those things. The thrill of the pursuit led to obtainment, and then I experienced a temporary feeling of satisfaction. It was a fleeting feeling and didn't last. A little like empty calories. They tasted good when going down, but ultimately, I was left with nothing but emptiness.

What I have discovered is that the whole time, I was actually in search of myself. And the whole time, I've been right here.

If you are asleep, you will miss it. You will miss the preciousness of the sacred moments that tick by. The whisper of the trees, the laughter of the children, the power of the reverence, and the awe you will feel by slowing down, becoming fully present, and being in your life NOW. The magnificence you can experience when you slow down and tune into you. Honoring the call of your Spirit, courageously following the breadcrumbs along a path that can only be lit from within.

Loving the Journey Allows Your Bloom to Fruit

By loving the journey, I have learned that the joy, the fulfillment, and the richness of life is found "along the way." It's in the uncovering and in the discovering of what really makes you feel alive, and it's in your willingness to step forward and be your true self. It's in the remembering of the truth of your Being, and it's in the knowing that your Soul came to Earth for the exploration, revelation, declaration, and expression of your Authentic Self, the Love that you are. *The journey is about how you are experiencing the life you are living, not where you are going.*

Have you ever wanted to embrace the spiritual side of your nature? Doing so means understanding that you are so much more than a body. You're more than your thoughts, feelings, behaviors. You are far more powerful than what you can even begin to imagine. You are a divine, spiritual Being, and the power of creation is available to you. You are here to wake up to your Original Wisdom, to the Love that you are. This recognition is the first step in falling into the flow of life and experiencing each of its succulent moments.

Consciousness Rising

Looking at your life as an experiment, as your own perfectly designed learning curriculum, shifts your perspective and allows you to know that everything is happening for your highest good, for your growth and learning, and for your expansion and expression. It's all for the discovery, the recovery, THE BIRTHING, and the remembering of who you truly are. Divine Love.

When you know that your thoughts create a powerful wave of energy that manifests itself into the physical world, you are given the motivation to take responsibility for the things going on in your own mind. Only you can take the responsibility of rewriting your play. Only you can rewire your old "programs"—the ones you have had enough of and that have played themselves out on repeat. This leads you to the decision to step forward, to harness your innate powers of creation, and to begin to envision what you want to bring forward and create in your life.

The magic is in the moments. It's not in the arrival to a particular destination. Your life is not over *there*; it's right *here*, right *now*. It's what happens along the way. It's being willing to take out a mirror and look deeply in your eyes and remember. Remember that all is unfolding as it should, that all is part of the grand plan, and that all that you seek, including your own Holy Grail, is inside.

Accessing and connecting to that wellspring of infinite Love— the God Source that is breathing life through you, that you are part of, that you are connected to, and that you are one with— is what life is really about. Your divinity is in there, in your humanness. It's buried deep under all the muck, all the misbeliefs, all the patterning, and all the bullshit, but it's in there. And it's waiting to be uncovered. It's waiting to be discovered. It's waiting for you. It's the AUTHENTIC YOU.

As Abraham, a group consciousness from the nonphysical dimension, so beautifully stated, "A happy life is just a string of happy moments. But most people don't allow the happy moment, because they're so busy trying to get a happy life."

Your life is in *this* moment. It's what is happening right here, right now. It's all around you. It is your breath and the rise and fall of your chest. It is the beating of your heart, the thoughts in your head, and the whispers of your Highest Self—your Soul, the Authentic You—being integrated into your life.

The journey *is* the discovery of your truth, your magic, your brilliance, your majesty. It's the recognition that despite all that you have been taught by the many influences in your life thus far, you are beautiful, brilliant, strong, resourceful, and alive. You are the sole creator of your life and your experience. You have all of the inner tools and resources you need in order to design a life that you love and that lets you feel alive and on purpose.

You Are an Emanation of Divine Love

In the Consciousness, Health, and Healing Program at the University of Santa Monica, Drs. Ron and Mary Hulnick describe entelechy in this way: "It is the entelechy of a human to realize itself as a pure emanation of Divine Love." I believe this is the purpose of our lives. In the discovery, in the letting go, and in the unfolding, I am likened to an apple blossom, gently, gracefully, and elegantly revealing myself. Then, over the course of my life, I learn how to stand as the fruit, in the fullness, richness, and luscious beauty that I am. Our lives are the unfolding of a divine journey. It is through this process of unfolding that one makes this discovery. The opening, unfolding, becoming, and Being of myself, of that unique flower, is the blossoming of my life and the realization that I am simply the pure essence of Love. Nothing more. Nothing less. This process, for me, will be fully realized only when I am done with this life, and even then...

With each part of the metamorphosis, my Light shines stronger, brighter, and fuller. I am aware that this awakening of consciousness will span my entire lifetime. The awakening into the understanding that I am, in fact, Divine Love. We are one. We, meaning you and me. We, meaning the collective whole. We, meaning you, me, and the Universe. In the oneness, I am humbled by the world around me, knowing it is mirroring who I believe myself to be. I am deeply grateful for this expanding consciousness, and for how the beauty of my life is elevated as I step forward into this unfolding. I am grateful for the compassion, the gentleness, and the tenderness in which I am able to hold myself. For the unconditional love, peace, and joy that I am able to experience for myself by just simply Being. There is no need to *try*; it is simply *being*. In this, there is Grace, Beauty, Humility, Compassion, Acceptance, Peace, Authenticity, Unconditional Love, and Original Wisdom. I am a spiritual Being having a human adventure. The essence and energy of Divine Love expressed in human form. In this reflection, my heart bursts with gratitude, and I am.

What Gifts Are You Sharing?

The gifts that you came here to share can only come through you. You are a unique, individualized expression of the Divine, an expression of Love, and an expression of God. There is no one on the entire planet that is expressing in the way that you are. Remember that this is the reclamation of your authentic empowerment. Are you standing forward as a leader in some way, either in your own family, community, industry, business, or world? Are you sharing your own unique expression through color, fashion, creativity, dance, or beauty? Perhaps you have the gift of gab, the skill to write poetry, the ability to create a garden, or the inspiration for a song. When you begin to believe this life is magic, it is. When you recognize the great influence you can have over your thoughts, beliefs, and actions—and thus the influence you have over your life as a divine creator—you realize you are here to manifest your heart's desires, whatever they may be, and to make the grand discovery of the treasure that is you.

As creators, we design our lives in ways that incorporate the lesson plans our soul came here to learn. Do you want to share your gift of seeing beauty in all things? Do you want to share your knowing that we are always surrounded by crystalline thought and magic? Do you want to share the gift of what you've learned about life through your own experience in a way that only you can?

Be in awe of the extraordinary life you live. Be in wonder of the miraculous masterpiece that is your life's adventure, with all its trials and triumphs, all its obstacles and opportunities, all its problems and possibilities. *And* all its miracles. Share your unbridled self to illustrate that joy. Fulfillment and aliveness are not to be discovered at the arrival of a destination; rather, you discover them along the breadcrumb trail that is leading you to *you*.

It is only through the unfolding of your life that you remember your wholeness. All of the pieces must come together so that you can revel in the beauty of the creative expression you are called to share. Share your gifts so others will do the same. Remember your Original Wisdom. In this mystical, magical, miraculous Universe, *you* are the love that you seek. Remember, your humanness is the individualized expression of All That Is. What a blessing that you're here! What a joy to witness how the divine shines through *you*.

Look at the Adventure to See the Exquisite Perfection

Let yourself marvel over the exquisiteness of the experiences in your life's adventure. Look behind you and lovingly honor the unfolding of your life. See the extraordinary perfection of it all. The beliefs you hold so close may be part of your own confinement. It is often through unhappiness and discontent that you delve deeper, walk farther, and risk bigger in the discovery of the fuller, richer, more multidimensional existence that is your life's adventure. The way the dots connect to bring you to where you are today is truly a miracle. When you really look through the lens of Love, I trust you will recognize this truth in your life.

Since I was a young girl, I have dreamed of writing a book (under my apple tree, of course). Over many decades, I tucked away my stories, knowing that one day I would string them together into the story of my life. As I have reflected over the past five years, I have suddenly realized that it has been during this short time that I have found the deepest wisdom of my entire life. The Original Wisdom that I am so enthusiastic about helping you recognize in yourself. The longer I'm on the spiritual path, the more I'm aware it's about loving my humanness.

Through my healing journey and awakening into the Love that I am, I am aware that the rising of my consciousness could only have occurred with—and through—all of my life's lessons along the way. Thank you, my divine, wise, compassionate Soul for unfolding my life's lesson plan. I honor the collection of this incredible adventure—the good, the bad, the ugly, and the super-wicked ugly. I realize that the expression of my Authentic Self—expressed through my human experience, guided by my Original Wisdom, makes a miracle out of me and my plain ol' extra *ordinary* life.

As it does yours.

And so it is.

Opportunity for Transformation
Take Action

This is the twelfth Opportunity for Transformation. This is your chance to take action and move your life forward, discover a new part of your consciousness, and create an experience for yourself that will deepen your learning of this material. All of the OFTs are designed to assist you in more fully integrating Original Wisdom from your Authentic Self into your day-to-day life. If you would like to download an actual worksheet or listen to an audio version of this OFT, please visit donnabond.com/opportunityfortransformation.

Identifying the Blessings of the Journey Thus Far

As you have engaged in the process of this book and taken action to delve into your own heart, you have likely discovered some splendid things about your sweet self. Reflect on them.

Become aware of your magnificence. Own that. *Be* those qualities, embrace your gifts, and allow them to lead your life. What are the gifts you came here to share, the ones that only you can express? Your unique, individualized expression that only you can bring to the world? That sharing matters because that is your expression of the Divine. Journal about this in the first person and then read it aloud.

I invite you to take these learnings and apply them to the way you are living your life. If you would like support in experiencing these concepts firsthand, you can learn more about doing so on donnabond.com.

Sacred Truth Activation

This is the twelfth Sacred Truth Activation. Find a quiet, private space to center yourself, light a candle, and speak these words aloud. If you would like to listen to an audio version of this guided personal decree, please visit donnabond.com/sacredtruthactivations.

I Am the Expression of the Journey

I am aware that my life is not a place to arrive to. I am aware that there are many perceived destinations that act only as pivot points along my life's journey. I am aware that my life is a miraculous unfolding. I am a miraculous unfolding. My life provides the path on which I can discover and uncover my true, essential nature, which is the energy of Divine Love, and only on this path can I blossom. I am aware that "now" moments comprise the whole of my life. I am aware that the more acceptance I bring to all of the moments, the more robust my experience. I engage and am fully present with each moment. I am in love with the unfolding of myself and my life. I love and revere all of the people, places, situations, opportunities, experiences, perceived wins, and cosmic redirections in the whole of my life. In all of it, I am grateful. I am discovering I am the expression of love in my life.

I am aware that the breadcrumbs leading me along the path are woven into the fabric of the landscape. I am aware that I am that landscape. I am the sun and the moon and the stars. I am aware that my life is a reflection of my consciousness, and the journey I travel is composed of the many parts that comprise the whole. I am aware that Love is intelligent, and my life is filled with the energy of this intelligence. I am deeply appreciative and grateful for all of the parts of my journey. I am aware that as a unique, individualized expression of divine intelligence, there is no other journey exactly like mine. I am aware that there is no other expression exactly like mine. I am empowered by my Authentic Self to direct my life in ways that bring me alive. I am aware that life is happening through me. Life is happening now. It is not out there, over here, or around the next corner. My life is in this moment, now. *In this knowing, I harness the power of my Authentic Self, I remember my Original Wisdom, and I come back to my center. I am fully present. In this act, I experience myself as the presence of Love—in Love, with Love, and as Love—and see my extraordinary life as the miracle that it is.*

Notes

A Course in Miracles. Glen Ellen: Foundation for Inner Peace, 1975.

Abraham, Esther Hicks, and Jerry Hicks. *The Vortex: Where the Law of Attraction Assembles All Cooperative Relationships*. Carlsbad: Hay House, Inc., 2009.

Abraham. Home of Abraham-Hicks Law of Attraction. Accessed October 30, 2020. https://www.abraham-hicks.com/.

Amethyst. "Herbs ~ Apple." Accessed January 11, 2020. http://spheresoflight.com.au/axismundi/index.php?page=apple.

Anka, Daryl. The Official Site of Bashar Channeled by Darryl Anka. Accessed December 11, 2020. https://www.bashar.org/.

Anoria. "Avalon, the Isle of Apples." Last modified July 14, 2019. http://woodbetweenworldsblog.com/avalon-the-isle-of-apples/.

Antanaityte, Neringa. "Mind Matters: How To Effortlessly Have More Positive Thoughts." Accessed January 11, 2020. https://tlexinstitute.com/how-to-effortlessly-have-more-positive-thoughts.

Appell, Elizabeth. "Risk Poem." January 1979. https://readelizabeth.com/.

"Apple." The Goddess Tree. Accessed October 30, 2020. http:// www.thegoddesstree.com/trees/Apple.htm.

"Avalon." Wikipedia. Last modified November 29, 2020. https:// en.wikipedia.org/wiki/The_Isle_of_Avalon.

Boyle, Lenora. "30 Self-Defeating Beliefs Common to Women." Last modified January 25, 2008. https://lenoraboyle. com/2008/01/30-self-defeating-beliefs-common-to-women/.

Brown, Brenee. Brené Brown. Accessed December 14, 2020. https://brenebrown.com/.

Campbell, Joseph. *The Hero with a Thousand Faces*. Princeton: Pantheon Books, 1972.

"Chalice Well." Wikipedia. Last modified August 4, 2020. https://en.wikipedia.org/wiki/Chalice_Well. (Chalice Well lid design by Frederick Bligh Bond. A possible reference to Excalibur, the sword of the legendary King Arthur.)

Chandler, Steve. "Steve Chandler's mp3 audio and mp4 video products." Accessed December 2017. https://www.ste-vechandler.com/audio.html.

Coelho, Paulo. *The Alchemist*. San Francisco: HarperOne, 1993.

Coon, Robert. Earth Chakras, Sacred Sites, and their locations. Accessed December 18, 2020. http://earthchakras.org/Loca-tions.php.

Dispenza, Dr. Joe. *Breaking the Habit of Being Yourself: How to Lose Your Mind and Create a New One*. Carlsbad: Hay House Inc., 2013.

Dyer, Dr. Wayne W. *Wishes Fulfilled: Mastering the Art of Mani-festing*. Carlsbad: Hay House Inc., 2013.

"Entelechy Definitions." YourDictionary. Accessed December 14, 2020. https://www.yourdictionary.com/entelechy.

"Fear: Definition of Fear by Oxford Dictionary on Lexico.com Also Meaning of Fear." Lexico. Accessed December 14, 2020. https://www.lexico.com/en/definition/fear.

Freeman, Jerry. "7 levels of consciousness: The path of enlightenment." Last modified November 17, 2014. https://tmhome.com/books-videos/7-states-of-consciousness-video-interview/.

Geoffrey of Monmouth. *The Life of Merlin: Vita Merlini*. N.p.: Forgotten Books, 2008.

"Glastonbury Tor." Sacred Destinations. Accessed December 18, 2020. http://www.sacred-destinations.com/england/glastonbury-tor.

Gwendolyn. "The Goddess Tree Grows *APPLE." Last modified September 3, 2009. http://sticksandstonescircle.com/profiles/blogs/the-goddess-tree-grows-apple.

Hawkins, David R., M.D., Ph.D. *Letting Go: The Pathway of Surrender*. Carlsbad: Hay House Inc., 2002.

Hawkins, David R., M.D., Ph.D. *Power vs. Force: The Hidden Determinants of Human Behavior*. Carlsbad: Hay House Inc., 2002.

"Hero's journey." Wikipedia. Accessed January 5, 2020. https://en.wikipedia.org/wiki/Hero's_journey.

Hicks, Esther, and Jerry Hicks. *Ask and It Is Given: Learning to Manifest Your Desires*. Carlsbad: Hay House Inc., 2004.

Hicks, Esther, and Jerry Hicks. *The Essential Law of Attraction Collection*. Carlsbad: Hay House Inc., 2015.

Hinkins, John-Roger. *Timeless Wisdoms Volume One*. Los Angeles: Mandeville Press, 2008.

Holden, Hollie. The Official Site of Hollie Holden - Mother, Writer, Soul Student, Love Advocate, Truth Lover. Here Are My Thoughts, Ideas and Wonderings about Life, Love,

Spirituality, Ups, Downs, Being a Mum and Everything in between... Accessed December 14, 2020. https://www.hollieholden.me/.

Holden, Robert Ph.D. *Authentic Success: Essential Lessons and Practices from the World's Leading Coaching Program on Success Intelligence.* Carlsbad: Hay House Inc., 2011.

Holden, Robert Ph.D. *Loveability: Love-a-Bil-It-y | 'luv biliti | noun: Knowing How to Love and Be Loved.* Carlsbad: Hay House, Inc., 2014

Holden, Robert, Ph.D. Robert Holden, Ph.D. Accessed December 15, 2019. https://www.robertholden.com/.

Holliwell, Raymond. *Working with the Law: 11 Truth Principles for Successful Living.* N.p.: DeVorss & Company: 2005

Holton, Gerald, and Stephen G. Brush. *Physics, the Human Adventure: From Copernicus to Einstein and Beyond.* New Brunswick: Rutgers University Press, 2001.

Hoomans, Joel. "35,000 Decisions: The Great Choices of Strategic Leaders." Last modified March 20, 2015. https://go.roberts.edu/leadingedge/the-great-choices-of-strategic-leaders.

Houston, Jean. Jean Houston. Accessed December 15, 2020. http://www.jeanhouston.com/.

Houston, Jean. *The Wizard of Us: Transformational Lessons from Oz.* New York: Atria Books/Beyond Words, 2016.

Hulnick, H. Ronald, Ph.D., and Mary R. Hulnick, Ph.D. *Loyalty to Your Soul: The Heart of Spiritual Psychology.* Carlsbad: Hay House, Inc., 2011.

Hulnick, H. Ronald, Ph.D., and Mary R. Hulnick, Ph.D. All lectures, Master's of Arts in Spiritual Psychology with an Emphasis in Consciousness, Health, and Healing. Accessed August 28, 2016. https://www.universityofsantamonica.edu/.

Hulnick, Mary R., Ph.D., and H. Ronald Hulnick, Ph.D. *Remembering the Light Within: A Course in Soul-Centered Living.* Carlsbad: Hay House, Inc., 2017.

Hulnick, H. Ronald, Ph.D., and Mary R. Hulnick, Ph.D. Ron & Mary. Accessed March 6, 2020. https://www.ronandmary-hulnick.com/.

"The Intuitive Mind Is a Sacred Gift and the Rational Mind Is a Faithful Servant." Quote Investigator. Last modified September 18, 2013. https://quoteinvestigator.com/2013/09/18/intuitive-mind/.

JD. "Great Tony Robbins Quotes." Accessed September 25, 2020. https://sourcesofinsight.com/tony-robbins-quotes/.

Lambdin, Thomas O., B. P. Grenfell, A. S. Hunt, Bentley Layton, and Craig Schenk. "Gnostic Gospel of Thomas Verse 70." The Gospel of Thomas. Accessed December 14, 2020. https://www.sacred-texts.com/chr/thomas.htm.

Lindberg, Sara. "It's Not Me, It's You: Projection Explained in Human Terms." Last modified September 15, 2018. https://www.healthline.com/health/projection-psychology#takeaway.

Lucado, Max. "Feed Your Faith, Not Your Fears." Accessed March 24, 2020. https://maxlucado.com/listen/feed-your-faith-not-your-fears/.

Mann, Nicholas R. *The Isle of Avalon, Sacred Mysteries of Arthur and Glastonbury.* London: Green Magic, 2001.

Morrissey, Mary. Author and narrator. "Life Coach and Personal Development Expert." "The Dreambuilder." Class lecture, December 14, 2015. https://www.marymorrissey.com/.

Moskowitz, Clara. "Fact or Fiction?: Energy Can Neither Be Created Nor Destroyed." Last modified August 5, 2014. https://www.scientificamerican.com/article/energy-can-neither-be-created-nor-destroyed/.

Myss, Caroline. *Advanced Energy Anatomy: The Science of Co-Creation and Your Power of Choice*. Read by the author. Louisville: Sounds True, 2001. Audio CD, approximately eighteen hours.

Myss, Caroline. *Intuitive Power: Your Natural Resource*. Read by the author. New York: Hay House Inc., 2004. Audio CD, approximately eighteen hours.

"Nikola Tesla." Maison D'être Philosophy Bookstore. Accessed December 14, 2020. https://www.genordell.com/stores/maison/Tesla.htm.

Price, John Randolph. *The Abundance Book*. New York: Hay House Inc., 1996.

Proctor, Bob. "Bob Proctor 'Happy & Grateful' Money Affirmation." Last modified January 6, 2015. https://www.highwaytoenlightenment.com/bob-proctor-happy-grateful-money-affirmation/.

"Projection." Good Therapy. Last modified February 16, 2016. https://www.goodtherapy.org/blog/psychpedia/projection.

"Quote by Albert Einstein." Goodreads. Accessed December 14, 2020. https://www.goodreads.com/quotes/1799-the-world-as-we-have-created-it-is-a-process.

"Quote by Henry Ford." Goodreads. Accessed December 14, 2020. https://www.goodreads.com/quotes/638-whether-you-think-you-can-or-you-think-you-can-t-you-re.

"Ralph Waldo Emerson Mind Quotations." QuoteTab. Accessed December 14, 2020. https://www.quotetab.com/ralph-waldo-emerson-quotes-about-mind.

Ray, King Godfré. *The "I Am" Discourses*. Schaumburg: Saint Germain Press, 1945.

Redfield, James. *The Celestine Prophecy: An Adventure*. Alabama: Satorini Publishing, 1993.

"Religion." Wikipedia. Last modified December 9, 2020. https://en.wikipedia.org/wiki/Religious.

Robert, Ohotto. "All Has Value." Class lecture, December 11, 2020. https://www.ohotto.com/.

Robinson, Ken, and Lou Aronica. *Finding Your Element: How to Discover Your Talents and Passions and Transform Your Life.* London: Penguin Books, 2014.

Rudd, Richard. *The Gene Keys: Embracing Your Higher Purpose.* London: Watkins Publishing, 2013.

Tolle, Eckhart. *The Power of Now: A Guide to Spiritual Enlightenment.* Vancouver: Namaste Publishing, 1997.

"We are not human beings having a Spiritual experience; we are Spiritual beings having a human experience."
This is attributed to Pierre Teilhard de Chardin in *The Joy of Kindness* (1993) by Robert J. Furey, p. 138. But it is attributed to G. I. Gurdjieff in *Beyond Prophecies and Predictions: Everyone's Guide to The Coming Changes* (1993) by Moira Timms, p. 62. Neither cite a source. It was widely popularized by Wayne Dyer, who often quotes it in his presentations, crediting it to Chardin. Stephen Covey also credits it to Chardin in *Living the 7 Habits: Stories of Courage and Inspiration* (2000), p. 47. Such statements could be considered paraphrases of Hegel's dictum that says that matter is Spirit fallen into a state of self-otherness. Or any number of thousands of similarly vague quotes by hundreds of predecessors. I am honored to join the legacy.

Wyss, Kathrin M. "How we support you." Accessed January 11, 2020. https://www.bizshaman.com/services.html.

Zukuv, Gary. Seat of the Soul Institute. Accessed December 14, 2020. https://seatofthesoul.com/.

Zukav, Gary, Oprah Winfrey, and Maya Angelou. *The Seat of the Soul.* New York: Simon and Schuster, 1989.

Acknowledgments

It is a privilege and an honor to be awake on the planet right now. I acknowledge *all* of the lightworkers, healers, intuitives, thought leaders, change-makers, optimists, and hope-holders; channelers, wisdom teachers, sages, mystics, yogis, white witches, enchantresses, goddesses, magicians, alchemists, and meditators; angelic, elemental, animal, and etheric realms; all spiritual teachers in their many forms; and consciousness leaders across the globe who are holding the Light every day for the global transformation of consciousness that is underway at this time. I am humbled and honored to stand with you.

My gratitude for Spirit is boundless and alive. The great mystery with which I dance daily has tirelessly and patiently waited for my attention with immense loving. I am humbled in the presence of this great and magnificent LOVE every single day, and I am beyond honored to be here working on behalf of the Light.

Drs. Ron and Mary Hulnick, co-directors and founding faculty at the University of Santa Monica, my deepest heartfelt gratitude, along with a deep bow, goes to you both for your exceptional work in Spiritual Psychology. I am forever grateful for the exquisite container of loving you have cultivated. Also, I am grateful for the thousands who are awake at this time because of your work. If our paths hadn't crossed, who knows where I would be today. I am deeply grateful for both of you. You are both models of peace and compassion.

To the University of Santa Monica staff, faculty, and volunteers; the Soul-brothers and Soul-sisters of the Spiritual Psychology Class of 2015; the Consciousness, Health, and Healing Class of 2016; the Soul-Center Professional Coaching Class of 2017; and the Soul-Centered Facilitation class of 2019, I have the deepest gratitude for all of the authenticity, the tears, the revelations, the support, the awareness, the learnings, the shedding, the loving, and the shared exaltation and joy of Spirit. Thank you for witnessing my revelation of my Authentic Self.

Dr. Robert Holden, my deepest well of profound gratitude goes to you for *not* pulling my name out of the hat! For inviting me to reach deeper and inquire further into myself. For demonstrating to me what it means to be the *presence of Love* on Earth at this time. I am beyond grateful for your guidance and your friendship, as well as for the gracious way you've shared your wisdom work with the world. Thank you for being on the planet at the same time as me. Thank you for writing the most beautiful foreword for my first book. So much love and gratitude to you.

James Van Praagh, you magic man—timing is everything— my deepest thanks go to you for having your spiritual arm around me, for your honesty, for your humor, and for redirecting me through the garden of Eden, inspiring Original Wisdom. Maybe Adam and Eve will make it into the next book!

John Hruby, for your brilliance, guidance, cheering, and fixing, I am eternally grateful. Thank you for seeing Spirit Girl and for making this project better!

Erin Ashby, thank you for really helping me take Spirit Girl out of the closet. Now let's invite everyone else to do the same!

Nancy O'Leary, director of education at USM, thank you for going back into the closed building during the pandemic to retrieve my manuscript. I am deeply grateful for the love, time, and attention you put into reviewing my book.

Such deep gratitude and thanks to the many, many authors whose teachings have become my trusted Soul advisors. When I hear or read your words, truth rings clearly inside of me in a way that cannot be contested. Though there are too many to name, I want to recognize a few of you amazing Souls. Gary Zukav, when I read *The Seat of the Soul* in 1989 on an airplane, I was literally coming out of my seat as the truth rang true in my Being. Since then, I've wanted to be a spiritual teacher. A nod to Michael Newton, Norma Milanovich, Dr. Brian Wiess, Penny Pierce, Esther and Jerry Hicks, Carl Rogers, Eileen Cady, Dr. David Hawkins, Cynthia Bourgeault, Mary Morrissey, John Randolph Price, Eckhart Tolle, Deepak Chopra, Dr. Wayne Dyer, Joseph Campbell, Dr. Joe Dispenza, and Bashar. The luminary Richard Rudd, I am humbled by your work. Caroline Myss, thank you for making me laugh and making me cry with all of your brilliance. I dream of taking you to lunch for an in-person chat one day.

Above all else, I continually extend my deepest gratitude to my own experience with the unconditional, Divine Love of God.

To *all* of my incredible clients—whether we have coached together one on one, you've been in one of my workshops or on a retreat, or we have yet to actually meet—*thank you* for giving me the opportunity to serve you so deeply. Thank you for allowing me to share my heart, my song, and the concepts I am so passionate about, and thank you for trusting me to be your guide during your journey of personal transformation. It is my honor and privilege to be a safe, sacred space of loving for each and every person Spirit sends my way. I am continually in awe of the magnificence of each of you, and I am deeply grateful for the opportunity to be used as a channel for the Divine, reflecting back the brilliance of your Love and Light.

Lara Asher, thank you for editing my book, and thank you for all of your support and encouragement along the way! From the moment we connected, we were drawn to work with each other. I consider it a divine appointment.

Grace Cavanaugh, thank you for your fierce love, thank you for awakening the strength of my inner goddess, thank you for calling forward the Divine Feminine within me, and thank you for helping me to remember my inner power and inviting me into my next level. I love you.

Bruce Brainerd, my sacred friend, thank you for being the catalyst for my spiritual awakening. Thank you for being my mirror and for showing me what excellence looks like.

Joanne Menon and Nicola Behrman, OMG! Can you believe this miraculous, Spirit-filled adventure we are on together? We've seen it a thousand times up close and personal, and we know for sure that *you can't make this shit up!* What a glorious journey we share together from different corners of the world. I am truly grateful for our strong Soul bond. Thank you for being there for all the counsel, all the tears, all the joy, and all the growth. You are my Soul sisters.

Lori Richards! Thank you for all of the deep contemplation, for sharing ACIM lessons, for the talks and the tears, and for the counsel and the guidance. *You* are exquisitely my positive projection, dear friend. Thank you for being in my life.

Johnna Trimmer, thank you for clearing my life path! For showing me firsthand the power of the invisible world. For inviting me to reclaim my health, my power, and my life. I am so grateful for you, and I love you.

Sara Harper, I adore you. Thank you for always being my biggest fan, for your encouragement, for the many opportunities you've invited me into, and for your constant support when I made the leap out of hospitality and into the world of being a spiritual teacher and coach.

Olga Peddie, thank you for choosing me as your coach! For being my very first paying client in a private coaching journey! For allowing me to be a witness to your incredible transformation and your reclamation of your Spirit and your aliveness. I love you.

Suri Sawyer, you bring an immense amount of joy, laughter, fun, lightness of being, and aliveness into my life. Thank you for who you are and for the magic you bring into our lives.

To my Spirit guide and father, Joe, and to my Earth guides, Betty, Mara, and Nicolle, it's my honor and joy to walk with you on the journey in this life. Thank you for being my family. I wish us more time to be together. I love you.

Paul Bond. You are my Wiiiiisssssssshhhhhhh. Thank you for finding me and making me your wife. For loving me no matter what. For showing me what it means to live on purpose. For being the great love of my life. Without you, none of my world would *be*. Thank you for being an exceptional mirror and for being my creative partner as we build our beautiful life together. And thank you for all of the versions of my beautiful book cover! I love you.

About the Author

Donna Bond, M.A., is a Soul-centered catalyst for personal transformation. Considered an Igniter of Light, Donna serves as an author, a speaker, a spiritual life and business coach, and a personal transformation consultant. Supporting individual transformation of consciousness, she helps clients across the globe evolve into new heights of meaningful success, personal fulfillment, and spiritual aliveness.

Donna offers inspiring classes, workshops, and transformative, in-depth life-coaching programs that help individuals and businesses unlock the full potential of their lives. A graduate of the University of Santa Monica, she holds a master's degree in Spiritual Psychology with an emphasis in Consciousness, Health, and Healing. Also, from USM, she has her Professional Coaching and Soul-Centered Facilitation certifications. After being a hospitality sales and marketing executive for twenty-eight years, Donna stepped down from her marketing role at The Ritz-Carlton and has since combined her business savvy and her intuitive, Soul-centered coaching and facilitation to offer a more meaningful contribution to the world.

Donna's heartfelt intention is to raise the vibration of the planet by helping people awaken into their true nature as spiritual Beings having a human adventure. With this purpose as her guiding mission, she assists others in leading more loving, joyful, authentic, and fulfilled lives full of meaning and purpose.

She and her husband, award-winning oil painter Paul Bond, live part-time in both Southern California and Costa Rica with their two cats, Mystic and Rumi.

AUTHOR • SPEAKER • COACH

Lets Connect

Find out more about Donna Bond:

Official Website
donnabond.com

Amazon
Goodreads

Facebook Official Page
www.facebook.com/DonnaBondProfessionalCoaching

Instagram
www.instagram.com/donnabondcoach

CPSIA information can be obtained
at www.ICGtesting.com
Printed in the USA
FSHW020724060321

9 781612 449555